"An inspiring, challenging, and front yard to Church Under the ... ... store. Combine that with a deep dive into wealth, poverty, and tools for community action and you will find that this is a handbook for practitioners and armchair supporters alike."

—**Mary Nelson**, *Interim President & CEO, Christian Community Development Association*

"In our nation and across the globe we are buckling under the weight of inequality. We see the eruptions in our cities and the devastation across our land. What to do? In *Commonwealth* we find the answer. Showing us the Christian principles and practices of community development that weave us all into the solution, Jimmy Dorrell outlines the clear path, both from experience and from careful biblical and social analysis. This powerful book is desperately needed. May we heed its wisdom."

—**Michael O. Emerson**, *Professor and Department Head of Sociology, University of Illinois at Chicago*

"Jimmy Dorrell is a prophet in both word and deed. *Commonwealth* challenges our very notions of a successful life. Jimmy points us to Jesus' teaching about living a full life, to give oneself over to caring for the impoverished, the common good, rather than simply acquiring more wealth and possessions for our own consumption. If we heed the wisdom of *Commonwealth*, born out of more than four decades of living and working in impoverished communities, our world would experience the promise of the true transformation of the kingdom of God."

—**Jeremy K. Everett**, *Executive Director, Baylor Collaborative on Hunger and Poverty*

"In *Commonwealth: Transformation through Christian Community Development*, Jimmy Dorrell does an excellent job of weaving the principles of Christian community development, biblical directives and his personal story of ministry and development. These all are extremely helpful for us in the church today. This excellent book is enormously important to be read by the church in these difficult days. For some reason the church has never been able to truly understand the poor and be committed to the biblical mandate of caring for them. Riches have often become the priority of too many Christians, and Jimmy goes a long way in guiding us and motivating us to be biblical in our lifestyles. I highly recommend Jimmy Dorrell's *Commonwealth*."

—**Wayne "Coach" Gordon**, *Pastor, Lawndale Christian Community Church and Professor of Urban Ministry, Northern Seminary*

"*Commonwealth* provides readers with an opportunity to recalibrate our moral compass, for without a plumb line, we know not from which we deviate, and all will deviate. Because we have a gracious and loving God, we are allowed a pathway back into relationship with him. I am grateful that with these words, Dorrell continues to challenge us to be honest about who we are in relationship to others, for that is what defines our authentic relationship with God."

—**Elizabeth Darling,** *former CEO and President, OneStar Foundation*

"How many of us can honestly say we've taken Jesus at his Beatitudinal word? Not just with our sermons and associations, but with our daily lives? Jimmy Dorrell is one of the rare ones who might be able to look God freely in the face—one whose testimony here convicts, clarifies, inspires, and confronts. For all those who sense there is more to Christ's Gospel than individual salvation and defending one's turf, here is a Jesus Way inviting your feet."

—**Anne Snyder,** *Editor-in-Chief,* Comment

"Jimmy Dorrell has taken nonapplied texts in his Bible Belt area and combined them with a vision for 'Church Under the Bridge' and partnered with underserved neighborhoods to transform Waco's 'Tale of Two Cities' into a 'Commonwealth.' Told with typical Jimmy Dorrell gusto and deference, he has made the story of poverty alleviation into an ongoing art form."

—**Ray Bakke,** *Professor of Global Urban Ministries, Regent College*

Commonwealth

Transformation through Christian Community Development

Jimmy M. Dorrell

1845BOOKS

Cover and book design by Kasey McBeath
Cover image: customer of the Jubilee Food Market, a nonprofit grocery store
in a lower-income food desert in Waco, Texas

Library of Congress Cataloging-in-Publication Data
Names: Dorrell, Jimmy, 1950- author.
Title: Commonwealth : transformation through Christian community
    development / Jimmy M. Dorrell.
Other titles: Common wealth
Description: Waco : 1845 Books, 2020. | Includes bibliographical
    references. | Summary: "Outlines the traditional biblical and
    theological understanding of wealth, and issues a call for urban mission
    and reconciliation through examples taken from the work of Mission
    Waco"-- Provided by publisher.
Identifiers: LCCN 2020020813 (print) | LCCN 2020020814 (ebook) | ISBN
    9781481313506 (paperback) | ISBN 9781481313537 (pdf) | ISBN
    9781481313520 (mobi) | ISBN 9781481313513 (epub)
Subjects: LCSH: Wealth--Religious aspects--Christianity. | Wealth--Biblical
    teaching. | Poverty--Religious aspects--Christianity.
Classification: LCC BR115.W4 D67 2020 (print) | LCC BR115.W4 (ebook) |
    DDC 241/.68--dc23
LC record available at https://lccn.loc.gov/2020020813
LC ebook record available at https://lccn.loc.gov/2020020814

This book is dedicated to my neighbors, every one of them who taught me how to love.

After more than four decades living in the same house and sharing life in my neighborhood with hundreds of men, women, teens, and children, the stories and insights in the book are theirs and the principles I learned about the kingdom of God are from them.

- To Junior Craig, the chronic alcoholic who often passed out on our front porch;
- To David, my incredible friend of some thirty-five years who still mows my yard and laughs a lot;
- To Dennis, the mentally ill man who blew his mind on drugs years before;
- To Libby, Janette, and the other woman who finally beat the streets after years of trying;
- To William, the older man who frequently sang "My Girl" to my wife;
- To Damon, the fatherless kid with the filthy mouth, who after years of prison still hugs me today;
- To Steve, the humble can collector driven to daily recycling by his addiction;
- To the hundreds of kids on our basketball court learning to play together;
- To Dixie, who frequently came battered to our door after a beating by her boyfriend;
- To Johnny, the Elvis look-alike, who had an opinion about most everything;
- To Gilbert, the "scrapper" who collected and sold thousands of almost worthless items;
- To "Preacher Ed," who used a huge speaker on his car to invite residents to Bible study;
- To Johnny, the teenager who went to war in Iraq, but was killed there on his second tour and his dad who never got over it;
- To the beat cop who genuinely cared more about the criminals than their crimes;
- To Dorothy, who died of sickle cell and lost her son to prison and suicide;
- To Jackie, Marchel, and Bonnie, who lived in a condemned house just a block away;

- To Lisa, the always happy children's director for Mission Waco;
- To James V., the overgrown, temperamental man with a little boy's mind;
- To the schoolteachers who were underpaid and under-resourced with below grade-level skills;
- To Lolita, who still lives in the housing projects and loves watching WWE wrestling;
- To the Lara family and the Ruiz family, who traveled different paths;
- To Carolina, who lost her little Angel to cancer when she was just six years old;
- To Brenda, suffering from cancer and kidney failure, who rode her wheelchair through the neighborhood while singing Christian songs;
- To Stevie and other young men who overcame the odds and became remarkable men;
- To Joe, who could sing like an angel, but who stole my lawnmower more than once;
- To Hugh and Lisa, Joe and Nancy, Brad and Sis, Jerry and Dail, and Ed and Rita for their shared Christian call to live incarnationally in a poor and diverse neighborhood;
- To Simona, a woman in a wheelchair who nevertheless created our first neighborhood watch;
- To Jason, Angel, Marnie, Randy, Scott, Megan, Jeni, Musiki, Etta, Allison, and the other young adults and college students who moved into the neighborhood to make a difference;
- To the sixty-five other adults and students who lived in our big house with us over these years;
- To those who remodeled or built houses and moved to share life in a diverse neighborhood;
- To my international neighbors of thirty years, the Mendozas and Sister Inez in Mexico City, and Gee St. Vil, in Haiti.
- To my own adult children, who grew up in this challenged neighborhood, yet embrace it as their own still today;
- To my wife of forty-four years, who loved our neighbors like no one else ever could;
- And to all the donors outside the neighborhood who believed in us and still do.

CONTENTS

Illustration by Stacy Williams

PREFACE

W hen I began writing this book, the U.S. economy was still surging. Wall Street was breaking records, unemployment was very low, and the wealthy were reaping the blessings of an unprecedented time. Even nonprofits and churches who helped the poor were doing better.

Then "the wheels fell off." Early in 2020 the COVID-19 coronavirus surprised the United States and another 184 countries of the 195 nations in the world. With more confirmed illnesses and deaths still expected, a jaw-dropping number of cases had been reported globally by late spring, including thousands of deaths. America topped the death chart among all nations.

This global pandemic not only devastated families all over the world, but magnified hidden injustices that impacted the poor and marginalized. Seemingly a respecter of no class or race or age, even those blessed with social privilege and power became ill and died. But as months passed, data began to reveal that those living in environments that prevented social distancing, access to facemasks, and adequate healthcare testing were being hit hardest. The percentage of people of color, the poor, and the elderly, particularly those in nursing homes, skyrocketed well beyond the white middle class numbers. Of course, many of them were already at higher risk to infection because of a lifetime of untreated medical problems due to a lack of health insurance in our nation.

As often is the case, blaming the victim is a common push-back. "If only they had. . . . ," goes the argument. Despite years of growing affluence, few changes have occurred to uplift America's urban poor neighborhoods in the last several decades. Subtly ignoring systemic injustices in America's infrastructure is normative, even in our nation of wealth. As the rich get richer and more of the poor fall well below the federal poverty guideline, underlying structures and social injustices persist. Though the Preamble boldly proclaims, "We the people . . . to provide welfare for all," we have become a nation of "haves" and "have-nots."

Perhaps, as the economy restarts and things "get back to normal," the impact of the pandemic could be the catalyst to ask, "What changes can we make in our citizens and cities that would prevent the devastation in the next pandemic?" "How can we overcome health disparities in the richest nation in the world next time?" "How could we create an economy where the top percent reap the fruits of what could be shared with the majority of our nation?" The COVID-19 pandemic has highlighted so many of our broken or inadequate systems. Unemployment, low minimum wages, lack of affordable housing, and inadequate healthcare are only a few of the drastic issues facing the poor today in our communities. Racism still exists in various forms. Food deserts continue to grow. Gun violence and mass incarceration continue to infect our society. There are more.

One of the most notable issues to me during these months was the awkward silence of Christians during the epidemic. While those who lost personal rights voiced their displeasure, there were too few voices from Christians condemning the root causes of injustices experienced by the poor that were now exposed by the pandemic. Whether evangelical, mainstream churches, or charismatic denominations, few of them seemed to coalesce during these last several months with an outcry to focus on Christian community development to rebuild the broken systems we saw. Christ wept over the city, who healed the lame, the leper, and the mentally ill, and who fed the hungry. What will it take to engage our churches, Sunday School classes, and

Bible Study groups to feel what he feels and act like he would
act? Christians, by definition, follow Jesus. Even the new covenant calls us to focus on others first before we get blessed. "Also,
seek the peace and prosperity of the city to which I have carried
you into exile. Pray to the Lord for it, because if it prospers, you
too will prosper" (Jer 29:7).

This book is about that question and some tangible solutions.
Perhaps it will make you think about things that you may not
have recently considered. It may challenge some your own presuppositions about why you are "blessed," while others are struggling. It may even offend you at times. Yet, more than anything,
I hope it will encourage you to become a committed disciple of
the living God and find joy in giving your life away in ways you
never imagined.

Jimmy Dorrell
Summer 2020

INTRODUCTION

I t was not what most religious people thought would happen. Jesus met two rich men; one was a despised tax collector who took advantage of others because of his position of power, the other was a religious ruler who followed the Old Testament Law and sought the popular Rabbi to ask how he could receive eternal life. While to the reader the answer appears obvious, Jesus proclaimed that salvation came to the irreputable publican, while the religious ruler was turned away in sadness. Both of these encounters had to do with money and the futures of those who possessed it.

Jesus was often forthright, confrontational, and even brazen in his teachings about God's kingdom. He certainly did not seem to want his hearers to accept common norms that uplifted the rich and rejected the poor and marginalized. No one knew that more than the wealthy he confronted in the streets. To one, he demanded, "Go and sell everything, give it to the poor, and come and follow me." Yet to another he said with authority, "Salvation has come to this house." These two encounters led to opposite outcomes that some would argue were even unfair or judgmental. Did Jesus hate rich people? Did he exclude the rich from entering God's kingdom? Why did his teaching suggest that the materially blessed may not go to heaven?

Most likely you are rich, especially by biblical standards. According to the Old Testament Law, if you had only one coat and a lack of money for food for your family, you were considered poor. Even most poor Americans live better than these standards, and the middle-class are considered rich by comparison. The truth is almost all Americans are far more financially blessed than 1.2 billion of the world's inhabitants living in "extreme poverty" at $1.90 a day and half of the world's poor who exist on $2.50 a day.

Most conversations about the disparities of economics seem to focus on how the poor became poor, as if their choices are primarily at fault for their condition. The more important question that needs to be asked is: why are the wealthy rich? Profound inequality of wealth, globally and nationally, raises theological, sociological, and practical questions that should be addressed. Are the poor really at fault for their own condition, or could it be that the financially wealthy are complicit with their economic condition? If true, what changes does God expect from the materially blessed?

Since it is such an important and foundational topic, the Bible addresses issues of wealth and poverty in ways that can be offensive to the rich. Material wealth bears heavy expectations, especially if you consider yourself a Christian. Even more than that, it has some inherent encumbrances and ignored warnings that have eternal impacts. The religious, rich young ruler turned away when he realized Jesus' words were too costly for him to follow him. The rich man who ignored the poor man in Jesus' parable was eternally condemned. The "goats," who did not see or respond appropriately to the needs of the poor and marginalized, were sent to eternal punishment. Ananias and his wife, Sapphira, lied to the Holy Spirit and fell dead for their deceitfulness about money. First John questions these Christians, saying, "If anyone has material possessions and sees his brother in need but has no pity on him, how can the love of God be in him?" (1 John 3:17). In John's Revelation even the Church at Laodicea, which saw itself as rich and needing nothing, was rebuked for its duplicity and called "wretched, pitiful, poor, blind and naked" (Rev 3:17).

Unfortunately most Western Christians ignore these incriminating biblical words or reinterpret them to fit their own personal context. Many so-called "Christians" have never read them or heard a sermon about the burden of wealth and its consequences on them. No one likes to hear damning words that impact their lifestyles and choices, especially when financial blessings have undergirded privilege and luxury. Timothy, the Apostle Paul's son in the faith, predicted, "For the time will come when people will not put up with sound doctrine. Instead, to suit their own desires, they will gather around them a great number of teachers to say what their itching ears want to hear. They will turn their ears away from the truth and turn aside to myths" (2 Tim 4:3-4). While having money alone does not send someone to hell, the love of it can: "For the love of money is a root of all kinds of evil. Some people, eager for money, have wandered from the faith and pierced themselves with many griefs" (1 Tim 6:10). The Apostle Luke reminds his people that the absentee landlord, representing God, will return to punish his unfaithful workers when they least expect: "From everyone who has been given much, much will be demanded; and from the one who has been entrusted with much, much more will be asked" (Luke 12:45-49).

The lure of wealth can subtly "steal, kill and destroy" the very joy that God intended for all his people to experience, rich and poor. "Money can't buy happiness," most say, but why is it that God's people chase this addictive drug, always seeking more? Most Christians say that it is better to give than to receive (Acts 20:35) and that "God loves a cheerful giver" (2 Cor 9:7), yet the thorny snares of selfishness seem to wrap their way around good intentions and choke out the fruit of compassion and generosity for others. True wealth is embedded in relationship and community. Studies have shown that the physiological joy generosity brings to a donor when giving to the needs of others means more than gaining more possessions. Jesus was not angry at the rich; he was disappointed that they were missing the mission of God's kingdom on earth. When Jesus demanded that the rich young ruler "give it all away and follow him," it was not punitive at all, but an invitation to come enjoy life fully through blessing others.

We Are Rich

According to the Wealth-X Billionaire Census 2019, there are over 2600 billionaires among sixty-six nations of the world. Globally, there are over 46.7 million millionaires who own approximately 44 percent of the world's wealth. While the United States has more wealth than any other country, other nations are increasing the number of millionaires. While many of these millionaires are philanthropic, many give hoping only to be recognized for their philanthropic legacy.

In 2019, the richest 10 percent of the world owned 82 percent of global wealth. The top 1 percent of the rich alone owned 45 percent. Shedding light on this inequality of distribution, *The Credit Suisse Global Wealth Report 2019* notes that "nearly half of the world's entire wealth is in the hands of millionaires." At the same time, "nearly one-third of American households, 29 percent, lived in 'lower class' households," the Pew Research Center said in a 2018 report.

In 2018, just over 38 million Americans, about 11.8 percent of the nation, struggled below the Federal Poverty Guideline, determined as $25,100 a year for a family of four. In 2019 the threshold is $25,750. According to the Bureau of Labor Statistics, it costs on average $20,194 per person per year to live. The average cost of living for an American on average is $53,046, though standards in cities and states can vary widely.

Ironically, "Americans believe it takes an average $2.3 million in personal net worth to be considered wealthy." That's more than twenty times the actual median net worth of U.S. households, according to the Federal Reserve's Survey of Consumer Finances released in 2017. "More than half of Americans are optimistic that they will be wealthy at some point in their lives, and two in five believe they will achieve that goal within a decade. Eight percent say they already consider themselves wealthy, although their numerical definition of wealth is lower—they believe they achieved wealth at almost $700,000 in net worth" (Schwab's 2019 Modern Wealth Index Survey).

It is easy to condemn the rich as arrogant and greedy. But the symbols of their affluence like expensive cars, yachts, private airplanes, stylish clothes, and lavish vacations often hold a lure even to the average American. The reality is that material possessions affect all of us, not just the ultra-rich. Even the poor can be materialistic and driven by sheer greed to buy clothing, jewelry, and items that hurt their budgets.

How we define, use, and think about money becomes a volatile spiritual arena of good and evil, requiring reflection, discernment, and action for those who want to heed the truths of the kingdom of God.

This book is not intended as a sentence to hell for being wealthy. The rich are important to God as are all of his creations. They have their own problems in life even with so many physical blessings. The rich get sick, get divorced, struggle with addictions, and may have maladjusted children. The problem, though, is that riches may hinder their ability to hear and know God, but nonmillionaires can also lose their spiritual vision as well. Almost anyone "has two coats" and cannot see the pain of the poor and marginalized. Poverty of spirit is the common call to rich and poor and a requirement in God's kingdom. The problem is that wealth silently and aggressively blurs the vision of the possessor and can prevent them from comprehending eternal matters. The chapters ahead will explore profound examples expressed by Jesus, which must be understood to comprehend the gravity of his perspective on economics.

In the City, for the City . . . "Common-Wealth"

A commonwealth is a voluntary group organized to promote and strengthen cooperation and advance economics, social development, and human rights in member organizations. The British Commonwealth consists of fifty-three nations that loosely organize themselves in a free association to build constructive relationships. Healthy cities can be similar kinds of commonwealths in purpose as local government, schools, churches, nonprofits, neighborhood associations, businesses, law enforcement, and other entities voluntarily come together to create communities that thrive and bless all their citizens.

Their commonwealth is much more than tax dollars; it is the collection of gifts that each entity brings to create God's *shalom* ("well-being"). When various entities freely meet, dialogue, plan, encourage, learn, volunteer, and address areas of concern, the community becomes healthy and interdependent. However, when those same groups only seem to care about their personal issues or cannot find time for the common good, community dysfunction follows.

The commonwealth of a city must always include both the rich and the poor to hear each other's concerns. Unfortunately, both economic classes often do not meet, nor really listen to one another.

Most of the financial resources of our cities, nation, and world are owned by a relatively small number of people. As the gap between the rich and the poor widens in the United States, fear between classes increases. Prejudice, misunderstandings, and blame toward other groups are frequent in communities that are segregated by race, ethnicity, location, and class. As a result many of our cities are struggling more than ever to get diverse populations together to discuss challenges and share both the financial and human capital needed to heal our communities. The deeper healing of our neighborhoods and communities requires the commonwealth of all residents.

Specifically, we need churches at the table. While the good news is that more and more churches seem to have members volunteering in their local communities, very few of them are engaged at the systemic level where critical decisions are made that affect the whole community. Most churches have wealthy believers who know how to run board meetings, make policy, and influence politicians in their daily lives. Yet few of these people engage in city council or civic boards unless issues arise that personally affect them. Even more important is the engagement by committed Christians who can bring a Godly perspective to community decision making. These representatives must be able to sit at tables with other community leaders who do not share their values and may hold other worldviews. Christians are called to be the salt, yeast, and light in the whole community, not segregated to Sunday morning enclaves which ignore the issues of their city. The call to transform the community has strong biblical roots.

Churches rarely donate to "secular" needs that impact their neighborhoods, especially churches that are under-resourced. While many churches struggle to stay within their budgets, giving would encourage them to make some financial investment in their cities. Not only would beautification projects in distressed neighborhoods uplift residents who live there, funding for projects that address crime, underperforming schools, and community blight can be a powerful testimony of "good news" to residents who view churches as self-centered and inward focused.

Even following years of living in the depression of Babylon's captivity of Judah, long after losing their homeland and temple, God's prophet, Jeremiah, says, "Also, seek the peace and prosperity of the city to which I have carried you into exile. Pray to the Lord for it, because if it prospers, you too will prosper" (Jer 29:7). He challenged them to plant gardens, share food, marry and have families, and invest in their new foreign home. To bless their new home would bless them. The accumulation of wealth is first for the community and its residents, not for the gaining of individual wealth. If the community prospers, everyone prospers. Unlike traditional paternalism which sprinkles small portions of the bounty of the rich to the poor at the end of a good year, the priority of the materially blessed is to help build infrastructures in their communities and pathways that give all residents the opportunity to flourish. God's *shalom* is relational and says that seeing and responding to the needs of our neighbor—the hungry, thirsty, naked, estranged, imprisoned, and sick—is basic to the city's salvation and prosperity. Furthermore, the selfless generosity of genuine sacrifice for my community saves the rich from the thorns which destroy the fruit of the Gospel.

Wealth is to be shared, not hoarded. "From everyone who has been given much, much will be demanded; and from the one who has been entrusted with much, much more will be asked" (Luke 12:48). And when, not if, you give, beware of pride that seeks attention. Unlike philanthropy that sometimes seeks personal recognition, the Christian model of giving is based in humility. "But when you give to the needy, do not let your left hand know what your right hand is doing" (Matt 6:3).

In the chapters ahead, principles and practices of Christian community development will be highlighted as a significant way that resourced Christians can invest in the prosperity of their own cities, nation, and world. Based on the New Testament's teaching that all of God's people are endowed with spiritual gifts to be used in building God's kingdom, everyone has a place and expectation to participate. Some are gifted to make money, but others have equally important gifts. Some Christians are skilled at planning, organizing, communicating, teaching, encouraging, or praying. All these different gifts are needed to help our cities prosper.

Discipleship Is a Journey of Real Living

How people steward their money is a reflection of their faith and ethics. But even for a committed Christian that redistribution is challenging. Releasing the tight grip we have on our lives and discovering the joy of selfless generosity requires detoxification. Addiction to material wealth, privilege, worldly power, and attention requires transformation, often taking years to change. Similar to the twelve steps in Alcoholics Anonymous, release from this "narcotic soul poison" (Walter Rauschenbusch) requires more than an admission of entrapment. It requires honest confession, accountability, courage, forming new habits, and seeing behavioral change in others. It also takes enough humility to know that there are "triggers," which can unexpectedly cause relapse. It also requires deeper relationships with those who model simplicity and relate to the financially poor.

Growing behavioral changes lead to humble actions that address those who are "hungry, thirsty, strangers, naked, and in prison" (Matt 25:31-46). New insights, understanding, and experiences over time remove the myopia that clouds godly vision. History is filled with examples and seekers of God who have addressed issues of wealth and poverty. This is a biblical issue that fills the Scriptures. The Law, Prophets, Wisdom Literature, Gospels, Epistles, and even the Revelation of John all have profound words about a proper and healthy understanding of the blessings and warnings of both riches and poverty. Because of the importance of these recurring themes, the early Christian writers also had volumes of books that addressed them. Augustine, Aristotle, Aquinas, Ignatius, Martin Luther, John Calvin, the Reformers, Radical Reformers, and various orders of monks all wrote profound treatises or books about the ways followers of Jesus should regard the lure of wealth and the care for the poor. The Anabaptist, Puritans, Catholic, Orthodox, and Protestant denominations have all discipled their adherents to follow moral and ethical teachings based on their views of the Scripture.

Unfortunately, Christians often do not understand basic principles of real helping. Rather than temporary relief, more and more Christians are understanding the benefits of empowerment and Christian community development models that engage those in need as part of the answer to their own problems. Job training, microloans, asset-based community organizing, nonprofit grocery stores in food deserts, ridding payday and predatory loans, and participant engagement deepen dignity and pride for and within changing neighborhoods. Listening to the opinions of the poor who struggle to survive on minimum wage or cannot find affordable housing helps the rich to genuinely hear and respect those who are struggling. In many cases the skill sets of the wealthy, including advocacy, legal, political, and financial knowledge, become even more valuable in distressed neighborhoods than financial donations. Mobilizing churches and existing nonprofits to think and act in a deeper and more fruitful way can impact communities in need.

Financial Wealth and the Loss of Joy

I wish I could have been at Zacchaeus' house the day he met with Jesus to see everyone's faces when he announced his commitment to give away half of his income and quadruple his financial returns to those he had cheated as the chief tax collector in the area. Jaws must have dropped. Squeals of astonishment and bursts of clapping must have filled the house. I would love to have heard Jesus then say, "Today, salvation has come to this house" (Luke 19:9).

Zacchaeus' decision to give back to those in his community impacted the whole city, particularly those with few resources.

While nothing is known about what actually happened in the months and years that followed Zacchaeus' astounding conversion, I choose to believe that the community was changed in significant ways. The poorest of the poor must have had enough food in their homes to feed the whole family. The potholes in those gravel streets were likely filled from new funds, and new jobs were created through the local government. Certainly new microbusinesses popped up selling fruits and vegetables grown in the once barren fields nearby. Several folks must have bought new donkeys with their returned taxes, while others repaired their dilapidated houses. The local doctor now had enough medicine to heal his friends in the city. There was even a new community fund for the widows and orphans. Zacchaeus likely stood on his porch looking down the hillside towards his community, smiled, and said, "This is real wealth!"

In the chapters ahead I have two main goals. One is to peel back the layers of deceit that cloud our vision of God's kingdom coming to earth. The other is to invite all of God's followers to experience the joy of being generous community builders who love their neighbors as themselves. As with Zacchaeus, this path requires seeing ourselves as God sees us and then discovering the joy of honestly confessing and repenting that you are serving mammon instead of God. The journey includes understanding the biblical revelation of God's order, interpreting within the context of significant historical eras and people regarding possessions, and from this adopting basic principles of Christian community development that impact our neighbors. With deep gratitude to God, I will share the joys of our story among the poor and marginalized with hope that you may discover your own path into your community.

1

SALVATION HAS COME TO THIS HOUSE

I grew up in a Christian home where the Bible was elevated above other forms of truth. I attended church, learned the Bible, and avoided the vices that were most abhorrent to practicing believers. I also learned God cared for the poor, at least I read that he did. But with almost no contact with the poor, the Bible's teachings about them remained quite abstract and irrelevant.

I was the shortest student in my high school, at least until my brother moved up a grade the next year. If being the shortest kid in those awkward teenage years was not hard enough, my peers constantly reminded me of it. Fortunately for me it was ten years after high school that the satirical song entitled "Short People," sung by Randy Newman, would hit the charts and add insult to injury. My newest peers seemed to think it was incumbent on them to sing it and remind me, had I forgotten, that I was short. They also enjoyed singing the portions like, "We don't want no short people round here," "Short people got no reason to live," and "Short people got nobody to love."

In the story from Scripture about Zacchaeus, his physical shortness was just one of his problems. As if the ridicule for his short stature was not already challenging enough, the diminutive Zacchaeus (Luke 19:1-9) was also the despised chief tax collector, a publican, among the Jews in Jericho. Though his name meant "pure," his peers saw him only as purely selfish.

As a Jew collecting taxes for the Roman government, he was viewed as a traitor and considered corrupt by his own peers. Tax collectors were known to be so corrupt that they unashamedly cheated their own countrymen to become wealthy. Sinners and tax collectors were synonymous in this context. No one liked tax collectors.

Climb Up to See: Seeking Requires Action

A rumor began to spread one day that Jesus was coming through Jericho on his way to Jerusalem, for what is now called Holy Week. These were the last few days of the traveling Teacher's life before he would be arrested, tortured, and crucified. For thousands of years, Jericho was known as an oasis town to tourists on their way to the feasts in Jerusalem. It was also known for its balsam. Years earlier, the same road led to the retreat palace of Herod the Great during the winters. It was the place where Jesus told the parable of the Good Samaritan who helped the man beaten and robbed. And now the city was clamoring to see the miracle worker who had just healed blind Bartimaeus, the persistent beggar.

As in most tourist towns, crowds gather quickly when news spreads of a celebrity coming to the village. Zacchaeus, the local chief tax collector, heard the rumors and wanted to see this Teacher who had performed miracles and confronted the religious Pharisees. Whether from curiosity or a deep desire to see a prophet who could reorient his meandering life toward a better path, he hustled down to the Jericho road. But alas, the crowds were already packed onto the dirt roadsides and the short tax collector could not see anything. No Jew was about to move over for the tax collector. Yet successful publicans get things done, so Zacchaeus ran up the road a few more yards to access the only option that seemed plausible. With sandals off he crawled up a large sycamore tree and found a limb that was just right above the road. As the dust on the road rose higher, he watched and waited among the throngs of common folk, merchants, government officials, and religious leaders. The onlookers murmured, yelled, clapped, and even ridiculed the small band of disciples as they grew closer. And then there he was. Jesus and his disciples were just below the tree.

Come Down to Be Seen: Intimacy Requires Vulnerability

"Come down immediately," the Teacher said, as he looked up at Zacchaeus. "I must come to your house today." "Was he talking to me? What did he say?" the publican must have thought. As Jesus focused his eyes clearly on him, Zacchaeus now knew it was him. Realizing this, the small man scurried down the large tree, his hands and feet scraped and scratched from sliding down the trunk, with confusion and excitement that he had been chosen.

The crowd murmured as Jesus reached out to touch Zacchaeus with a gentle gesture of kindness. This was a shocking response by Jesus, especially since Zacchaeus was a rich tax collector who worked for the Roman government, which meant he often cheated the local residents with added taxes for their own pockets. As they began to walk up the hill to the tax collector's home, the murmuring among the crowd grew louder. "He's gone to be a guest of a sinner. How could a true prophet of God have the audacity to engage with such a short, little scoundrel as that man?" they screamed. The crowd did not approve of any invitation to share a meal with such a despised tax collector, and they began to wonder if this prophet was a real prophet like everyone said. They hissed and booed as Jesus and Zacchaeus walked up the trail to his beautiful home, paid for by their taxes.

The spontaneous lunch meeting must have caught Zacchaeus' family and neighbors by surprise. While they left their sandals outside the door and quickly washed their feet before entering the house, a servant boy was sent off to buy bread and wine for the guests. After receiving greetings by the Rabbi on the foreheads of the family, Jesus sat down on the open floor as the disciples joined them. "Shalom to your household. May God's peace be yours," Jesus said. And the conversation began. Since Jesus knew the heart of the publican and there was no need or time for pretentious words about the weather and the tourist trade in Jericho, Jesus' presence likely initiated nervous confession by Zacchaeus. There is no record of excuse making or blaming others for his underhanded work for gain. Zacchaeus understood that Jesus knew him, his motives, and his idolatry of wealth and possessions better than he did. Amidst conviction and shame, Zacchaeus blurted out, "Lord, Lord! Here and now I give half of my possessions to the poor, and if I have cheated anybody out of anything, I will pay back four times the amount" (Luke 19:8).

As the words gushed forth, the tax collector must have experienced the joyous feeling of being honest before God for the first time. After years of guilt about taking advantage of others, Zacchaeus heard himself say repentant words that would be costly. These were not words of cheap confession by a sinner in the presence of a "holy man." They came from the core of his soul, which had revolved around money and wealth for so long. The things that he loved the most were now confessed to Jesus as idolatrous gods that had taken him away from his life purpose to be a true son of Abraham. Now he wanted to know God more than he wanted anything else.

Real confession is hard for anyone, especially since justifying oneself is a natural trait for all humans. Confession that opens one's soul up in front of others is frightening and requires vulnerability. Saving face, blaming, excuse making, and delayed confrontation are normative for all sinners and religious Pharisees. As the Spirit of God deeply convicts those he seeks, our rare moments of honest reflection offering the choice to agree with God about loving other gods more than him quickly get diluted. Like Peter who swore allegiance to Jesus during the last meal they had together before the Lord's arrest, the later shame after repeated denial of Jesus cuts to the core of our being. It is hard to admit that we are liars, hypocrites, double-minded, and hard hearted. It is hard to confess that what we considered "little sins" of compromise, deceit, lust, and greed eventually emerged as the primary purpose and driver of our being. "I'm not all that bad," we contend, and the lies continue to be covered up.

Zacchaeus got quiet, his own words of repentance screaming in his ears. He must have almost laughed inside, astounded that he finally had the courage to say out loud what he knew was true. He must have felt fear wondering what Jesus would say. Then with piercing words of truth that almost no one could have imagined, Jesus said, "Today salvation has come to this house, because this man, too, is a son of Abraham. For the Son of Man came to seek and to save what was lost" (Luke 19:9-10).

There must have been a pregnant pause throughout the room. No rich man during Jesus' ministry had ever been declared saved in the kingdom of God. Would the rich really be able to enter it? Clapping by the disciples in the background may have broken the silence as they heard Jesus' powerful words. Surely there were smiles and hugs around the room. The reality that this tax collector was now a follower of the Living God filled the room with awe and wonder. Short people do have a reason to live . . . the song was wrong!

The Whole Gospel

I grew up in the evangelical culture that emphasized conversion experiences. We had tracts, revivals, evangelism training, and door-to-door efforts to talk to neighbors about being "born-again." Every sermon in church ended with an invitation to the unsaved to come forward and receive Christ. In those years, the powerful global impact of the Billy Graham Crusades was celebrated by churches as thousands of attendees would walk forward, prayerfully confess their sins, accept Jesus as Lord and Savior, and then be recognized as new believers. Some were baptized but few joined local churches.

Over the months and years ahead, however, many onlookers began to wonder what had really happened to them other than an outwardly religious experience. Often it seemed that the new Christians would slide back into old patterns of living just like the days before their experience. Though a few attended churches occasionally, gave a few dollars for the offering, and were generally polite to others, a transformation of their values and goals never seemed to take root. Repentance, the biblical word for turning around and going the other direction, was lacking in their supposed regeneration process. Discipleship appeared as optional for the ones who took it seriously, but not nearly as important as the one-time decision to "get saved and go to heaven."

"Salvation" in my evangelical world meant to describe the experience of committing to God, which includes the assurance of going to heaven someday. Yet the biblical word is so much more than bowing one's head and praying "the sinner's prayer." It is a threefold concept: "was saved" from my sins, "will be saved" for eternity, but also "am being saved" from the sins of my present life. In my evangelical world, the latter sounded too much like salvation by works, or being good enough through daily actions to earn heaven. But nothing could be further from the truth. The book of James, written to second generation Christians who seemed to be less enthusiastic about their faith than the first generation, urges these lackluster believers by saying, "Therefore get rid of all moral filth and the evil that is so prevalent and humbly accept the word planted in you, which can save you. Do not merely listen to the word, and so deceive yourselves. Do what it says" (Jas 1:21-22), and then, "In the same way, faith by itself, if it is not accompanied by actions, is dead" (Jas 2:17). Good works certainly do not save us, but without question there is no such thing as real faith that does not exude action. They are integrated words in the holistic Hebrew culture. Being and doing are parts of the same salvific experience. To say we believe something that is not accompanied by evidence of that belief is a lie. "If one of you says [to the brother or sister without clothes and daily food], 'Go, I wish you well; keep warm and well fed,' but does nothing about his physical needs, what good is it?" (Jas 2:16). God's grace of salvation produces fruit in keeping with repentance, John the Baptist preached to the outwardly religious Pharisees and Sadducees coming to him for baptism in Matthew 3. Luke said to all the Jews that having Abraham as their forefather is not enough (Luke 3:8). "Anyone who has two shirts should share with the one who has none, and anyone who has food should do the same" (Luke 3:11). Real repentance demands confession and action.

The Cost of Being a Christ Follower

In the century after the resurrection of Jesus, many of those Christians who fled west from local persecution were influenced by the Greco-Roman world. Plato's idea that the "soul" was distinctively separate for the whole person was different from the Hebraic worldview. Christians mistakenly separated body and soul. Unlike the biblical worldview where body, soul, and mind are all integrated, Gnosticism's metaphysical approach separated these. The Greeks believed that people could be "spiritual," unrelated to their human actions. Even today Christians frequently think of their spiritual life unrelated to their human actions. Such a belief is heretical according to the history of the Church and biblical scholarship. God cares about the whole person equally—physical, mental, and spiritual. What we do now on earth matters, even how we eat, drive our cars, and take care of our bodies, which are a "temple of the Holy Spirit" (1 Cor 6:19).

In the presence of Jesus, Zacchaeus stood up in his house and renounced his earthly possessions. Then Jesus affirmed his salvation. Never in a million years would my evangelical culture have published an evangelistic tract that included giving away one's possessions as one of the four steps to accepting Christ as Savior. Instead they would put an asterisk mark on the tract suggesting that this story was a unique situation only for the tax collector types to get saved. In my culture the often quoted "four spiritual laws" had nothing to do with the "physical laws" that included my possessions. Yet how is it that Jesus would not request of us, the wealthiest of the world, the same that he did of Zacchaeus, if not more? John's Epistle does. "How can you, rich Christian, ignore the needs of the hungry, poor, and marginalized and think you are Christian?" (1 John 3:17).

Unlike the rich young ruler who walked away sadly because selling all he owned and giving it to the poor was too great a cost, Zacchaeus discovers God's salvation. "Having said good-bye to all his possessions, he has become Jesus' disciple, successfully passing through the eye of a needle into God's kingdom, and acquired inexhaustible treasure in heaven" (Metzger 2007, 178). There would be a cost to follow. "Like Jesus' disciples, now he too can expect to exit on the periphery of society and endure criticism and insult" (179). While it may seem at first that Zacchaeus was seeking Jesus, it turns out that Jesus was seeking Zacchaeus. He was lost in a maze of overconsumption, stockpiling, and depriving others of the most basic provisions. Having repented of his wealth and committed to giving it away, Jesus' ministry is empowered to continue among the disenfranchised through redistribution and need meeting, even to the blind man healed earlier in Jericho.

Escaping Cultural Christianity

The journey begins with our own pilgrimage to "see in the mirror dimly" the distorted worldviews we embrace as a twenty-first century Pharisee, shaped mostly by cultural religion and preoccupation with being "people-pleasers." As "good kids from normal homes," our worldviews were shaped by Christian America, living out the inherent values of the culture. We are from two-parent, middle-income, neighborly households with good schools and a swimming pool. We went to church, sang the National Anthem, and played with other children who looked like us. Janet played the guitar and rode her horse. I played Little League baseball and made "A's" in school. Life was good.

What I never really saw was the racism of my community, divided by black and white, poverty and wealth. There were two schools at each grade level to separate "us" from "them." We played in different Little Leagues, were separated by race on the balcony and main floor of the only movie theater, and even drank water from the "white's only" or "colored" water fountains at the hamburger cafe. It was "normal" life. High school years got confusing. Vietnam was escalating. Hippies were growing long hair and talking about free love. The Beatles sang about "trips" without ever leaving home. Dr. Martin Luther King Jr. was marching with thousands against racism.

At age seventeen the rumors spread one Sunday morning that the "Negroes" (and other racist nuances of that name) were coming to our all-white church to join in the worship service as a statement that they were equals and that the world was changing. Most all of us were afraid about what that could mean for our safety. To alleviate our fears the deacons assured us that they would not let them into the church. They announced, out loud and without apology, the distorted social value of our culture right there in our big church, the supposed representative of the radical Jesus who called us to oneness.

The Black churchgoers never came, but something happened to me that day that has never gone away. While I too was afraid like my peers of what I did not understand, deep down I wondered why we Christians were not welcoming. Were we really trying to protect "God's order" of separating people of color with the dominant white culture, or as some said, could it be that the church itself had become complicit in the cultural norms? Despite the biblical words of being ministers of reconciliation that we discussed in Sunday School class weeks before, it was exposed as a façade and made impotent by our visible actions. As a teenager trying to grow in my faith and still respect my elders, I did not have the critical thinking skills then, which I am still embarrassed about today, to speak up. The blend of "Christianized" cultural norms and the teachings of Jesus were diametrically opposed.

Periods of awakening, small and large, have slowly remolded our viewpoints and lives. From a Calcutta slum to a decision to move into an impoverished, racially diverse neighborhood in Waco, Texas, Janet and I have come to see the world and our purpose in it differently than we did during our upbringing. The chapters ahead are a testimony of our slow obedience to God's kingdom that continued to chip away at the false presuppositions we formerly embraced. Gradually we discovered the joys of having relationships with the poor and marginalized in ways we had never known before. Unfortunately, we also have continued to discover more of the embedded views that often have hurt and disempowered the very ones we came to love.

Out of thirty-one parables that Jesus told in the synoptic Gospels, nineteen of them had to do with the misuse and distribution of wealth, social class, indebtedness, and worker pay. In addition, the encounters and teachings of Christ and the writings from the early church deepened Jesus' teachings and expanded upon the actions expected of the church. The Good Samaritan, the Rich Young Ruler, lepers, beggars, prostitutes, widows, and the socially rejected became powerful stories of the kingdom of God. We also discovered the high priority that the Christian Scriptures placed on a biblical view of wealth and poverty. Other passages in both Testaments highlight the corrosive impact of worldly wealth on spiritual maturity and holistic lifestyles. While a few of these acknowledge that wealth can be a tool of blessing others, many more of them point to the deceptive self-justification and vanity that often accompany riches. The following chapters will explore these biblical teachings of the Gospel writers decrying the soul-stealing potential of wealth. It will also look at historical journeys of well-known Christians who have sought to understand, explain, and adjust their own lives in light of biblical teaching. Looking through the lens of psychology, social behavior, and addiction to physical wealth, other followers will provide insight into the negative impact of economic distortions that are easily glorified in our Western culture and even steal the souls of those deemed "successful."

Over the years, we have "climbed a few trees" to evaluate our lives and see Jesus from a different viewpoint. We have confessed a lot of wrong views and actions. Some of those decisions developed as we matured, while others came through intentional decisions we made along the way.

In my early college years at Baylor University, I became a youth director and worked for five years in Waco at a local Baptist church. It was a meaningful invitation to hang out and impact teens, particularly the unchurched students at the local middle and high school campuses. Over the years we had weekly Bible studies that grew large, retreats that fostered deep relationships and spiritual reflection for teens, and numerous activities that drew friends of friends to the ever-growing youth group. I was now a "successful" youth minister and young academic who knew enough theological words to impress others.

One day I received a phone call from a local African American pastor, who also happened to be the president of the Waco NAACP chapter. His call was a plea for me to bring my all-white youth group to his part of the city to lead a vacation Bible school. He invited me to meet him at his church, St. Mary's Baptist Church, in "No Man's Land." Three questions revealed my small world. First, how could a Baptist church be called "St. Mary's," since it sounded much more Catholic than Protestant? Second, where in this city, one that I thought I knew well, was "No Man's Land" located? Third, but with a name like that is it safe, especially for a white boy?

In a mix of knowing what was right and fearing of possible newspaper headlines, I went. As I turned off the paved road toward his church, I was aghast. Houses that were falling down still had families living in them. Outdoor toilets were located just behind them. The dust of the graveled road could not hide the desperate poverty. "What am I doing here?" my mind screamed. As I pulled into the church, Reverend Pinckney met me. Before sitting down to talk details he suggested we walk the neighborhood and meet some of the residents. Children ran to meet him, moms waved, and unchained dogs barked just behind us. We stopped in front of an old house that literally leaned and had a small tree growing through the front porch. "May I look in?" I asked before waiting for an answer. As I slowly pushed the stuck door open, a man screamed, "What are you doing in my house?" Fear and surprise evoked nervous words of apologies from my mouth. "I didn't know anyone lived here. I am so sorry. Forgive me." As my eyes adjusted to the unlit room, only then did I notice he had not even seen me at all. Mr. Sparks was completely blind. He could not see me, the uninvited intruder, or the rats and roaches scurrying around the blighted house amidst smelly piles of molding clothes and garbage. Hurriedly I pulled the misshaped door closed behind me and quickly ran to the dirt road where Pinckney stood. He just smiled, reveling in the lesson learned by the white Pharisee from the other side of town.

In the next hour, the Baptist pastor showed me the open field behind the church where we would hold the five-day Vacation Bible School, and then he introduced me to a church member who would direct it along with my youth group. He also shared with me his dream to get the adjoining municipalities on both sides to incorporate the blighted island between them so they too could have running water, paved roads, and police protection. As the head of the NAACP, he understood his role of influencing other community leaders and pastors to consider advocating for them. Probably for the first time in my life, I saw dimly through the eyes of an African American pastor who loved his congregation and his neighborhood and wanted for them what most others already had.

Something happened to me that day. I was reluctantly exposed to poverty and segregation from the other side. Questions haunted me. How was it that a blind, seventy-six-year-old man could live in the squalor of a falling down house without utilities, only a few miles from where others lived with all the amenities of life? How could families in this day and age have to use outside toilets when my family had two and a half bathrooms with warm water? Why were poor African Americans segregated from "the good life" of the white world where I lived? As a Christian, how could I ever learn to advocate for the underserved and under-resourced like this pastor fighting systemic injustice stacked against him?

Jesus Came to My House

There is something transformative about climbing a tree above the chaos and patterns of normal daily life. A climber in a towering tree can see for miles in various directions, unimpeded by street level life. Instead of being pushed around by the crowds and their self-centered worlds, the view from above offered Zacchaeus the big picture. It is often in those unplanned experiences that the daily patterns, the entrenched opinions, and the people-pleasing efforts of life are minimized and pushed aside to make room for the bigger questions of life. Who am I? What is the purpose of life? Is my worldview anything more than a bunch of futile words that do not impact my life at all? Do I really care about God's will?

"God is a rewarder of those who diligently seek him" (Heb 11:6). Yet he also seeks those of us who are hiding in trees behind our excuses and fears. He calls us to take the road less traveled, seek the Creator, and trust that the scales will come off to see God and his ways more clearly.

That day in "No Man's Land," I saw more of myself than I had ever seen before—and I didn't like what I saw. I was a privileged white boy that viewed the world through the tainted lenses of my culture and religious past. I had to admit that I was prejudiced against others who were poor and not of my race or cultural background. I had shown favoritism, even though the Scripture clearly states, "If you show favoritism, you sin and are convicted by the law as lawbreakers" (Jas 2:9). I had "hoarded wealth," "insulted the poor," and "shown special attention to the man wearing fine clothes." I was a hypocrite and could no longer justify myself.

As hard as it was to begin breaking the chains of outward religion and racism, I experienced a growing liveliness that was exhilarating in my journey of faith. I knew that these were only two of many sins that needed transforming, some likely more challenging than these. Yet now the courage to take the upcoming pathways of discipleship seemed stronger and the call to the pilgrimage much clearer.

2
COMPASSION AND THE JOURNEY INTO PAIN

"Enter through the narrow gate. For wide is the gate and
broad is the road that leads to destruction, and many enter
through it. But small is the gate and narrow the road that
leads to life, and only a few find it." (Matt 7:13-14)

I n his classic book called *Pilgrim's Progress*, written in 1678, and
now in over two hundred translations, John Bunyan's allegory shares the journey of a man named Christian from "The
City of Destruction" (the world) looking for "The Celestial City"
(heaven). Christian is overwhelmed by the knowledge of his
own sin and wants more than ultimate destruction and hell. His
pilgrimage is filled with challenges, disappointments, doubts,
and distractions, but his call compels him through the trials of
life. Alone without his family, the protagonist meets numerous
characters along the way including The Evangelist, Obstinate,
Mr. Worldly Wiseman, Beelzebub, Vanity, Hypocrisy, Piety,
Wanton, Lord Hate-Good, Envy, Ignorance, The Flatterer, Much
Afraid, Atheist, and even Madame Bubble, who makes foolish
pilgrims so tired they fall asleep and never wake up. Each encounter is a unique scenario of the realities most all seekers of
truth experience in the journey of life.

The most profound lesson Bunyan teaches is that seeking
what matters most is a long and unknowable adventure that lies

ahead for pilgrims. Consequently, most people never choose to seek the allegorical "Celestial City" and settle in the "known world," with the masses who are spiritually asleep. Instead of seeking a life full of meaning and purpose into the unknown paths, they passively accept "normal life" and its perceived certainties. The wide gate of which the gospel writers speak is the easier path taken by most people. "If it is okay for the majority, it is fine for me," they posit, unwilling to journey down the road less traveled that leads to life and has only a few on the journey. With no serious understanding of life outside the presence of the loving God, they either unwittingly joke that if hell is where their friends are it is fine with them or they redefine salvation in man's terms, offering a nonbiblical form of cheap grace that includes everyone.

The Bible does not describe God as a passive Being who created everything and then moved on. In fact, it says just the opposite. God is a pursuer of those he created and loves. His desire is that all of creation be in his kingdom now and forever. The unique role of the Holy Spirit is to seek, call, convict, encourage, and send the created ones into the kingdom of God. "But seek first the kingdom of God and His righteousness, and all these things shall be added to you" (Matt 6:33).

Because genuine love always involves freedom to choose or reject God, humankind is wooed but never forced to come back to the loving Creator. Some outwardly reject God, others ignore him, and still others respond to his call, "Come to me, all you who are weary and burdened, and I will give you rest. Take my yoke upon you and learn from me, for I am gentle and humble in heart, and you will find rest for your souls" (Matt 11:28).

Those who are genuinely seeking God are "*rewarded*" (Heb 11:6) in their journey. Whether through cries to him in the night, reading the Bible or a Christian book, going to church, having discussions with Christians, or just being amazed at a beautiful sunset or millions of stars, seeking God is always met with his favor even though the journey may be challenging.

Around the World in 140 Days: Our Journey to Seek God

In 1982 my family took off around the world. After completing seminary and then taking a church job in the wealthier side of Houston, life had been good. Living in the suburbs in a newly built house that had the expected amenities, a safe neighborhood, successful neighbors that looked like us, and a community swimming pool all seemed like the goal. We landscaped our lawn and put up the expected privacy fence to secure additional isolation. But even with a successful job and lifestyle there was something missing. Janet and I had both walked through the narrow gate years before, agreeing that we would seek God and his direction at any cost. We could not find peace in the wealth of the suburbs that seemed so perfect to others. After long talks and fears of telling the newly made grandparents that we were taking their grandchild far away, we decided to sell our house and travel around the world, seeking God's will for our lives and serving the marginalized. With the purchase of our "open tickets," we put our possessions in a storage container, said goodbye to our family and friends, and began a four-and-a-half-month journey with our one-year-old in tow.

An open ticket meant we chose to travel without an itinerary. We spent weeks deciding which countries to visit, and what projects we might pursue and serve for as much time as we wanted in each location. With "wheels up," the jet propelled us onto a journey that impacted our lives forever. From New York City to Europe's cathedrals to the Berlin Wall we went. We traveled by Eurail to Germany and Italy and to our stay at L'Abri in Huémoz, Switzerland, the retreat center established by Francis Schaeffer for those who had lost or damaged their Christian faith and were now asking the right questions to get grounded again. With the Western portion of our trip completed, we headed to South Korea, Singapore, Malaysia, and Japan, all offering us new insights into God and his world. India was the last stop.

The global journey and subsequent trips opened our eyes to the world that God sees every day. While we saw the age-old

cathedrals of Europe, we noticed they were now mostly empty as Western culture had become ransacked by postmoder-
nity. We saw the art of Florence, the catacombs of Rome, and
the atheism of Communism. We sat in a library nestled in the
Alps, listened to tapes, and read books by amazing Christian
thinkers and apologists. We sought out the world's most prolific church in South Korea and met Christians who prayed for
each day and sent missionaries around the world. We also spent
time in conversations with Muslims, Buddhists, and Hindus in
other nations, some devout and some nominal followers of their
faith. We saw the poor—lots of them. There were multitudes of
children who had not eaten, sick who had no medicine, refugees
sleeping in camps, and people dying from a lack of clean water.

On the last leg of the trip, since Janet was pregnant, I left her
in the incredible care of the L'Abri community while I headed to
India alone, a nation of 1.3 billion people. Janet and I later returned to this Hindu nation together. No other country impacted
us like this exotic land, home to both the beautiful Taj Mahal and
the world's poorest and most unreached people groups. It was
also the home of Mother Teresa, the world-renowned Catholic
sister who later became the icon of compassion to millions. After
a few days I headed to Calcutta to find her ministries and spend
some time volunteering. Upon arrival we wandered through the
red light and blighted district of Mother Teresa's Kalighat, the
"home of the pure heart." It was a former Hindu temple she had
acquired in 1952 that was converted into a hospice for the dying,
destitute, and sick. Each day the Missionaries of Charity would
attend to the severely sick while having volunteers wash clothes,
feed the bedridden, and do any requested chores. Each night
some of the sick would die. Each morning after early prayers, the
Catholic sisters would go in rickshaws to the train station to find
the beggars who were days from dying. As I watched their daily
routines for the "least of these," the women became my heroes
while they cared for the most vulnerable of the world, including

those in the nearby slums and the street children. They never seemed to complain and found ways to have a thankful heart in the midst of so much pain and suffering.

One day we asked one of the sisters if Mother Teresa lived nearby. As a matter of fact, we were told, she had just returned from speaking in the States and she lived very close. With a reverent fear, we walked to her small apartment and knocked on the door. She opened it and invited us inside. "How could it be," we whispered to each other, "that the Nobel Peace Prize-winning 'saint,' recognized around the world, would not have security and servants to care for her?" We were invited to sit down while she shared about her recent trip and asked about us. Once hearing our story, she looked into our eyes and said what she said to so many sojourners: "Go find your own Calcutta."

As we got up to leave, I looked down at her bare feet and noticed how deformed they were. There were many stories about why her feet were so misshapen, but it was clear she could not care less about appearances. She would never choose a pedicure or a pair of pretty shoes, especially if it cost money out of her ministry and away from the thousands of poor that she and the Sisters of Charity were serving each day. It was there that the verse I had heard for years had new meaning. "How beautiful are the feet of those who bring good news!" (Rom 10:14-15).

At the end of this stimulating, exhausting, and disturbing journey, it was time to go home to have the second baby and start over in our own culture. We had to make some hard choices about where to live and what to do in this next phase of life. For the first time, we felt detoxed from the affluence of America's addiction to stuff and knew we could not return to "the good life" in one of the world's most opulent nations. But we could live among our own nation's poor and marginalized. We could go back to America intent on living more authentically with the principles of God's love. We could go back as real neighbors. We chose to return to Waco, Texas, a city we knew well, but one that has twice the poverty rate of most American cities. After the blessing of a respite with friends, American food, seeing family members, and looking for work, it was time to put our convictions into practice.

Incarnation

For several weeks we looked for houses in lower-income neighborhoods. It was hard to find a real estate agent who dared to show a listed house in areas feared for their crime and poverty. Then an agent we knew called and said, "I think I have something you might be interested in, but it's got a lot of need." With one child in hand, and another "on the way," Janet and I met the agent in an old part of the city that had once been a "nice" neighborhood. As these homes, built in 1920, had aged and low-income African Americans moved across the river into North Waco, "white flight" ensued. The old homes were now being purchased by unscrupulous landlords who would cram several poor families and individuals into them regardless of the conditions of the house. It had become an area with growing crime, drugs, and lots of prostitution.

We drove to the large, 4000-square-foot, two-story house across the street from a bar called "The Chat and Chew." The old house was occupied by two mentally ill veterans on one side, a nineteen-year-old tenant upstairs who had a passion for bizarre wall paint colors and for posters of naked girls, and an older nurse known as "the cat lady." After being released from the Army for mental health issues, the nurse had made it her mission to collect stray cats in her one-bedroom portion of the old house we were considering. Over forty felines now lived with her and the smell verified the numbers. Lots of rats and roaches shared living quarters in the house as well.

"It's gotta good roof," said the agent, somewhat in humor since nothing else seemed very persuasive about the house. "How much?" we asked. "$12,500," she responded, "but we might get it down to $12,000." She did, and we purchased the house in 1977.

"Sometimes there is a fine line between faith and stupid," Janet and I often say. The discernment needed to know what is a genuine, radical call from God rather than one mixed with other agendas is challenging. It is especially true when that call goes against traditional and cultural norms. Moving one's family into a bedraggled house in a blighted neighborhood with a high crime rate goes against most every norm that middle-class families erect. "It's dangerous," some said. "Your children will be negatively influenced." "You can drive over there to help 'those people' without living there." The list continued, with almost no one applauding our decision. "That is just plain stupid!" said the most vocal. Janet's parents certainly had grave concerns.

"Now faith is confidence in what we hope for and assurance about what we do not see" (Heb 11:1). The writer of Hebrews goes on to recognize the men and women who did hear God's call outside the cultural expectations and followed. Noah, Abraham, Isaac, Jacob, Joseph, Moses, David, and others often experienced rejection and suffering because of their choices. While God commended them for their faith, "none of them received what had been promised" (Heb 11:39). In other words, faith was not recognized because of some ultimate victory, but because people of God acted on what was ordained by God.

"The Word became flesh and blood, and moved into the neighborhood" (Peterson, *The Message*, John 1:14). Janet and I came to believe that incarnational living among those we knew we were called to love meant taking a risk and moving into the "bad neighborhood" in faith that Jesus calls us to be among those we serve. After years of watching frequently misguided mission trips by middle-class Christians taking short-term journeys to other countries or into urban poor neighborhoods to "get those people saved," we had little patience for the lack of relationships, abundance of cultural blind spots, and enormous amounts of wasted money. While recognizing the value of short-term "exposure trips" that frequently open the eyes and heart, as well as powerful spiritual lessons gained by the "go-er," genuine ministry occurs in relationships. There is no better relational context that being neighbors.

While our exposure trip around the world had caused Janet and I to see what we did not and could not see before the pilgrimage, our vision was now clearing. Upon our return to the States, we remembered the hundreds of street children in Calcutta, the Muslims in Malaysia, the persecuted Christians in Eastern Europe, and the empty cathedrals in Western Europe. We even prayed differently. When friends asked, "Did you have fun?" there was no way to answer. It was the wrong question. While inspirational and eye-opening, it was hard to see much of what we saw.

When our family moved into the old, blighted neighborhood, our vision continued to become clearer. With the former tenants moved out, we began to work on the old house. Remodeling was hot and dusty, and our skills and financial resources were limited. Since we could not afford air conditioning in the hot Texas temperature, we used fans and the open windows, offering us a consistent view outside. With heightened awareness and uncertainties, our eyes and ears were attuned to our surroundings. In the middle of the night we could hear people arguing as they walked down the street. We saw an occasional fight at the bar across the street. The prostitutes hailed down cars just outside our window, hoping for a trick to provide income. Almost daily we heard Junior Craig, the neighborhood drunk, knocking on our door asking for something.

Yet we also saw the children playing on the sidewalk, mommas sitting in lawn chairs in their front yards in the heat of the day, and the old guys playing dominoes on the porch. Our eyes were hypersensitive to our surroundings in a way they had never been before, especially to ensure our own children were safe in this unfamiliar turf. We also knew we were the only white people in the neighborhood and were uncertain how everyone else saw us.

As we worked on our "new" home, Janet and I would often take time to meet our new neighbors. Unlike more wealthy areas, the lower-income folks were mostly outside instead of cloistered and isolated in their own homes. We were pleasantly surprised by their friendliness, even if they were unsure about who we were and about our motives. With our own children beside us, it was easy to connect with the scores of children near our home. In only a few weeks, our front yard became the chosen playground as Janet taught the children games, read stories, and offered refreshments. Some of the African American kids frequently touched her white skin or her straight hair since they had never been so close to an Anglo, especially one who cared for them. In only a few weeks, we began our first "King's Club," a weekly gathering for children with a variety of activities and Bible stories.

3

RELATIONSHIPS CHANGE EVERYTHING

God created us to be relational beings. In the West's indi-vidualistic culture, most Christians assume that one's rela-tionship with God is alone the essence of faith. Yet Chris-tianity is more of an "us" than a "me." When Jesus was asked the greatest commandment, he replied, "You shall love the Lord your God with all your heart and with all your soul and with all your mind. This is the great and first commandment. And the second is like it: "You shall love your neighbor as yourself. On these two commandments depend all the Law and the Proph-ets" (Matt 22:35-40). In other words, we cannot have a genuine relationship with God without including our relationships with others. Biblically they are integrated into one.

As we moved to our cross-cultural neighborhood, we were clearly aware that we were neophytes when it came to under-standing how to build healthy relationships among the poor. We knew just enough to avoid the traditional trap of being "fixers," "givers," and "advisors" to those who were materially poor. Yet we knew there were others who had gone before us, locally and globally, who could teach us how to become genuine friends to our new neighbors.

Principles of Christian Community Development

Soon after our move, we met a woman who heard about our
call to the urban center of the city. She commented that she had
heard of a national group who had an annual conference around
similar ideas. Knowing we were novices who could certainly
learn from others, we found the Christian Community Development Association (CCDA). They too were a young organization
created in 1989 after gathering in Chicago to learn from each
other about loving the poor as well as discussing the challenges of addressing poverty, injustice, unemployment, addiction,
poorly performing schools, and crime in their communities.
Hungry to find peers who understood us, we joined their Denver conference in the early nineties. There we found the friends
we needed. Hearing from speakers and workshop leaders like
John Perkins, Wayne Gordon, Robert Lupton, Mary Nelson,
Glen Kehrein, Shane Claiborne, and others, we bonded with
them around common issues in which we all were focused. We
heard principles of relocation, redistribution, and reconciliation.
We were challenged to employ Asset Based Community Development (ABCD), helping meet basic needs. "A pure handout is
almost never appropriate, as it undermines the persons' capacity
to be a steward of his own resources and abilities" (Corbett and
Fikkert 2009, 102). We heard testimonies of lives and attitudes
changed and relationships transformed among blacks, whites,
and browns. We learned from others the creative ways they had
overcome unhealthy relief efforts attempted in the name of development and empowerment. Most of all we found a new group
of friends with shared vision for our cities and God's kingdom.

Relationships are the basis of any legitimate ministry, especially urban and cross-cultural ones. Based on my experience,
impoverished people seem to have a uniquely powerful gift of
discernment that can spot a fraud in a minute. They can usually tell when someone comes to manipulate them, proselyte
them, or give items away to them as a "project." It did not take
long for our new neighbors to trust us and believe we were
there because we cared for them—they could see it in our eyes

and in our actions. Since we determined our model of compassion would be built on empowerment instead of relief, our new friends felt respected.

When someone did ring our doorbell to ask for help, the decision was built around a conversation instead of a rule of order. We sometimes provided food, a ride, and even a few dollars to some, but not all. We learned from the neighbors who were the "takers," manipulators, addicts, and irresponsible. We learned that, no matter how impassioned the plea, every problem was not a real crisis. Since nothing ruins relationship building quicker than becoming the local philanthropist, Janet and I often had a list of small jobs around our house that those in need could do to receive help, making them an active part of their own solution. Sweeping the sidewalk, mowing the yard, picking up trash, and taking out the garbage gave those with needs the dignity of participating in the solution. Within months the neighbors knew that "the white people" were friends, but not easy prey for quick fixes. While we have occasionally been used, confused about what to do in certain situations, or discovered we did not make the right decision, appropriate generosity was still our guide. We found that giving indiscriminately can do more harm than good as well as undermine relationships, which every parent knows. Instead our motto became, "The people with the problem must be a part of the solution to the problem." Real charity is more than giving away money or stuff. A dollar given to a homeless man on the corner does not give time for discernment and relationship building. If the sign holder's problem is addiction, the dollar given enables the disease to continue unabated. These lose-lose encounters usually promote beggary and contribute to a loss of dignity if money is given, or guilt if the wealthy driver passes by and ignores the person. It is hard for the wealthy to know when to give. Relationships help overcome that confusion.

The Basketball Court

Besides owning a large, dilapidated, and inexpensive house, the vacant lot beside it came with the purchase. Though we had a little extra money from my job, due to the costs of house repairs we barely scratched out enough money that first year to pour a square slab of concrete and erect a basketball goal on the lot. An older neighbor who knew the skills of the job volunteered his time. By the time the cement was dry scores of young teens showed up to our half court to play. We obviously never imagined how popular our new addition would become. Throughout the next few years, we expanded the court two more times as money became available, until there was a full court and fence to keep the basketballs out of the streets. With a few rules, including no alcohol or drugs, the court was open to everyone until nighttime. Other than monitoring some occasional bad language and a few players with tempers, the kids created their own rules. Over the years thousands of children, youths, and adults have come, and still come, to the basketball court. We have tournaments, children's games, and other activities there. Ministry started without a building and on a shoestring budget.

For several years the basketball court and our front yard were the sole sites of our fledging new ministry, usually done after work in the afternoons or on the weekends. We rarely received outside financial help, but the growing list of volunteers from the community and Baylor University were invaluable resources. These volunteers allowed us to add a youth version of our children's program with activities beyond basketball.

Mama Came, Too

Frequently the mothers of the neighborhood children would come over to the basketball court to check on their child. Moving into their neighborhood made these connections natural. Through Janet's continued efforts to get to know these moms and other women in the neighborhood, a women's group was started to encourage them and provide a respite from their overwhelming lives. In those meetings the silence of their pain was broken. Some of the women quietly shared their struggles of physical abuse, indebtedness, struggles with their children at school, and even hunger of the whole family. Some asked for ways to help their husbands or boyfriends to receive job searching assistance. Others sought direction to get alcohol and drug abuse recovery for a family member. Unpaid bills led to utility cutoffs. Rent houses without insulation led to cold nights or extreme heat. Exhaustion, unhealthy diets, and constant demands compounded the ability to make wise choices with few resources. Yet at the women's group there was a place to laugh, talk, learn, hug, and be accepted just as they were.

Janet discovered most of the women felt that they had lost control over their lives and circumstances. Disempowerment is a common characteristic among lower-income adults who experience frequent failure or setbacks in an affluent culture. Yet one of the basic building blocks of change comes from the confidence that personal choices and ownership of decisions lead to a better life. Blaming others, feeling victimized, aloneness, fear, and ignorance can debilitate anyone from a healthy life. The women's group was the perfect environment to explore faulty thinking and create hope for change.

It also required winnable victories. As a growing group of middle-class women joined Janet and the neighborhood women in these gatherings, they began to set achievable personal goals and were often held accountable for their own choices. Whether they decided to eat better, read to their children, clean the house, or exercise once a week, there was now a caring mentor who would ask if they had accomplished their own goals. If the goals went unachieved, there was no rejection or blame, only more encouragement to try again. Change is hard enough and virtually impossible without an atmosphere of encouragement and hope to try again. The women who lived in poverty would rarely, if ever, break self-destructive patterns when belittled.

More than just the need for personal change was that of neighborhood change. Poor neighborhoods easily breed hopelessness. Trash in the yards, broken windows, decaying buildings, pothole-filled streets, crime, underperforming schools, and unruly crowds outside convenience and liquor stores breed downward spirals of community health. Yet many

disenfranchised neighbors are unaware of the power they possess to enact change. Many give up calling the city to get the
potholes filled, frustrated that those on the other side of town
get immediate response. The police are often slow to respond
to the petty thievery or loud music in the middle of the night.
Underpaid teachers in the inner city often feel hopeless with
too many students, a lack of resources, and constant battles
with parents who have disruptive children. Poverty is more
than a lack of resources and money, it is also about systems
which fail the impoverished repeatedly.

On one occasion the women's group was told that it was our
city's responsibility to put a streetlight at the end of each block in
order to deter and reduce crime. There were numerous corners
without light poles, and if there was one the pole had no working
light bulbs. Their streets were dark and cars were frequently van-
dalized. Janet, along with some of the other women, decided to
walk door-to-door on those blocks to ask residents to sign a city
petition to get their promised light. While many of the residents
felt it was a waste of time, they still signed. With pages filled with
signatures, a few of the women joined Janet on a trip to City Hall
to drop off the petition, knowing it would be several days until
they heard anything. They waited and then waited some more,
long past the deadline. The more cynical residents resorted to
the classic phrase, "I told you so!" They seemed correct in their
conclusions.

The word "power" (*poder*) in Spanish means "to enable." Unlike the "power over" definition, we embrace a "power from behind" model that helps empower others. When the teachable
moment occurred, Janet declared to her neighborhood friends,
"We're going back to City Hall!" They squeezed into several of the
volunteers' cars and headed downtown. Once inside the doorway
of the office where the petition was first delivered, Janet said, "Ap-
parently, we have been overlooked. Why didn't we get our light
on our street?" The receptionist said, "We've been really busy late-
ly and are behind on several things. We'll get to it in a few days
and give you a call." Having heard these dismissive excuses before,

Janet said with a quiet, but cold stare, "We are not leaving until the petition is found and approved!" With those simple words, an unforgettable lesson was learned by women who had never seen such strength displayed without an emotional tirade.

Two weeks later the neighbors gathered for a party on North 13th Street. The women had made refreshments and placed them on a table with chairs arranged around the new light pole at the end of the block. Earlier that day they watched the electric company climb a ladder and connect the wires to the new light. As dusk encroached on the daylight that evening, something big happened. A new light flicked and then dispelled the growing darkness on the corner. A roar of excitement accompanied it as neighbors shouted, "We did it!" For the next thirty minutes, a celebration erupted under the light pole. Indeed "they" did it.

4
JUBILEE BREAKS OUT

As the small ministry grew, friends asked if they could donate to our work. The answer was yes, but there was no nonprofit structure in place to provide the tax incentive for giving. In 1992 we created a small board of directors and incorporated Cross Cultural Experiences as a nonprofit organization to highlight both our out of country exposure trips in the world's poorest regions and our weekend-long intensive poverty simulations. Because the name was confusing to others, years later we changed it to Mission Waco/Mission World. The year after creating the nonprofit, a Christian foundation called Christian Mission Concerns decided that this empowerment-based model of community ministry was worth supporting, at least for a year. After the initial grant, I was able to leave my job as program director at a local social service agency. I joined Janet full-time to volunteer my efforts toward revitalizing our old, historic neighborhood, which had plunged deep into blight through the years.

Repairers of Broken Lives

Christians are called to be repairers, restoring God's world "on earth as it is in heaven" (Matt 6:10). The prophet Isaiah confronted the hypocrisy in his time of outward religion and "chain of injustices" toward the poor and marginalized. For example, he confronts the emptiness of religious fasting while quarreling and exploiting one's employees, not sharing food with the hungry, not helping the wanderer, or pointing fingers at others. He reminds them that good news to the poor includes freeing captives and helping the brokenhearted. It also involves "rebuilding walls" and "renewing ruined cities" (Isa 61:4).

The next steps were natural. Since the neighborhood residents were now friends, there were frequent opportunities to listen to their concerns. With a growing sense of power, numerous ideas about next steps were proposed. It seemed clear to most that job training and job finding assistance were priorities since legal financial resources were few. Jobs would bring money and a sense of dignity. However, like almost every program that Mission Waco has established through the years, we did not know much about how to accomplish what was requested and needed most by our friends. Assuming that "if you can Google it, you can do it," simply starting was the key. We knew that our new programs would need to mature over time, but there was no need to bring in a consultant, send leaders away for training, or let the unknowns that lay ahead immobilize us. With a little research and a few phone calls, we began a small pre-employment work maturity class to build foundational skills for our unemployed neighbors. This decision meant getting work documents together, such as birth certificates and Social Security cards. We taught and emphasized the basics, such as daily attendance, bus routes, punctuality, and how to correctly complete an application, build a resume, and do a successful interview. Often using roleplay and video playback, we stressed proper dress in the workplace and how to successfully deal with conflict with supervisors and coworkers, sometimes going over a particular skill multiple times so that a certain level of mastery was gained. They worked on G.E.D. skills such as reading and simple math. Incentives were often used to celebrate successful completion of each milestone. Field trips to local employment sites outside of fast food restaurants opened the eyes of the students to new workplace opportunities they never imagined. The group went to the local community college to hear from counselors and financial advisors who assured them scholarships could be found. They even toured a local bank to learn about getting their own account instead of being ripped off by check cashing predators. With weeks of practice, some of the class found employment, even if it was low paying, part time work. Each time someone was hired we celebrated and took pictures. Each event gifted power to those who had previously felt so powerless and incapable. Each paycheck instilled more dignity.

Repairers of Broken Walls

Throughout the years Mission Waco has bought and remodeled sixteen old buildings. Most all of them needed new roofs, HVAC systems, asbestos abatement, surveys, building permits, and a hundred other things to meet city codes. While seminary educated me in theology, it certainly had not prepared me to be a remodeling expert. Christian community development pushed me deeper into the construction world. There I discovered two lessons. The first was that I needed the expertise of laborers. The second was they needed us community developers to understand the role of Christians caring for the poor. Had it not been for the owner of the largest construction firm in Waco volunteering to help renovate the Jubilee Food Market, the nonprofit grocery store would never have been completed. He knew every subcontractor in town and unashamedly asked them for quality work at a discounted rate. His wife had heard of the project for the poor neighborhood and wanted him to help. As the general contractor, I watched his heart come alive during the renovation process as he asked questions about Mission Waco, the empowerment model, and why the poor and marginalized did what they did. As a good Catholic, he believed helping people in need was good, yet the idea of relationships, job training, and offering dignity to those in need were foreign concepts. The more he watched our staff relate to the neighborhood the more he embraced our call and methodology. He became our best advocate in the wider work world that knew little about our model of ministry. Four buildings and many years later, that general contractor is still helping. There are at least fifty other contractors who are also now friends and supporters of our work in the city, all because Mission Waco ventured into their world in order to help the poor. The widening circle of influence from those outside the "church world" has been remarkable as Mission Waco moved into the whole city with the whole gospel.

In the "program-based" world I grew up in, successful ministry was generally tied to having a building or ministry headquarters. With this expectation came the encumbering cost of sustaining the building through financial resources. However, we had learned that some of our best ministry occurred in the yard, on a playing field, or under a tree in a housing complex. We also learned that buildings are secondary to a philosophy of ministry. In our new world, we discovered that poverty was so much more than a lack of resources. While many of our neighbors were financially poor, the issues which kept them poor were often systemic and structural.

The rarely read book of Leviticus offers some insightful ideas about how injustice is to be addressed and implemented. The Year of Jubilee, written in God's Law, was to occur every fifty years. At the end of seven sabbatical years, all real property should automatically be given back to its original owner. Alongside this, those who were impoverished and had sold themselves as slaves to their brothers were to regain their liberty. The Old Testament Law recognized that because of generational poverty, new beginnings were needed. As in the New Testament church, new "wineskins," or models of ministry, were needed to deal both with structural sin as well as individual shortcomings.

As Mission Waco grew up, we realized that our ministry could never be effective if we did not deal with the injustices of structures that oppress the poor alongside providing empowerment ministries. As we acquired old, dilapidated buildings in the neighborhood, we often used the word "Jubilee" to communicate that our approach to change would be both programmatic and systemic.

Relationships and Christian community development take time. Well-meaning groups who often enter into under-resourced areas with hammers and paint brushes in hand often sabotage the natural process of effective urban ministry when they do things "for" instead of "with" the community in need. Yet as we deepened our friendships, the real issues and dreams were voiced by the neighborhood. "My uncle is struggling with crack addiction," a young adult shared. We knew our streets were filled with drug dealers who could sell an inexpensive "rock" for a quick "high" that temporarily overcame feelings of despair and inadequacy. We watched it destroy families, promote theft, and turn so many men and women into manipulators looking for their next fix. While we knew little about how to address the insidious problem of drugs and alcohol in our neighborhood, we knew that no action was unloving. A young staff member of Mission Waco, who had struggled with addiction as a teen and learned the importance of a good recovery program, encouraged us to consider opening a Christian-based recovery home. When the city of Waco donated a two-story, dilapidated old house just two blocks away, we jumped on the opportunity. Over the next several months, we found friends who had construction skills to help us stabilize the foundation, replace rotten wood, insulate the walls, paint the inside and outside, and build new steps. During the renovation we dove into the learning process of what was required to be an effective rehabilitation center and got the required permits approved. Finally, a seasoned recovery director, who had worked for a local agency, agreed to lead the effort in establishing community-based treatment.

Within the year Manna House was opened. The eleven-bed residential treatment program was open to local men from lower-income backgrounds. Funds were raised, intake policies and procedures were written. And one by one, men who had given up on themselves and any hope of change came to the door and were invited to enter the three-month Christian recovery program. Over the years hundreds of men have come. Many successfully completed the program, while others did not. Yet compared to most recovery programs, where relapse is still more common than sustained sobriety, the statistics at Manna House astounded us and defied normal programs. A few years later, we found our small program rated as the number one faith-based rehabilitation program in the state of Texas. Most importantly, broken men were finding life again in the neighborhood and returning to responsible lifestyles.

Most of the programs we created and the buildings we restored happened in that same way. "If we can Google it, we can do it," we said, gaining most of our strength and motivation from our neighbors who we now knew and loved. We studied, we listened, we experimented, and we called on our friends who knew more than us. While many of our professional acquaintances had little experience with poverty and disempowered families, they had vocational gifts we did not have. Contractors, accountants, and consultants recognized and affirmed our desire to bring healing and hope to an area of the city that had long ago been written off as "the bad neighborhood." Yet we knew these neighbors, the ones written off as predators and abusers. They were people just like us, trying to survive the scars of our past mistakes. They loved their children like we loved our children. They had dreams like we did. They wanted to change just like we want change. Of course there were those neighborhood residents in the "chaos" stage of selfish living, just like many of our wealthy acquaintances whose lifestyles are narcissistic and chaotic, still not ready or willing to walk the road less traveled toward a new life. Yet there were others ready to change, learn to read, be a better parent, get a job, and even volunteer.

In a Porn Theater

Six blocks from our "new" house was an old shopping center built in the early 1930s. In the early days, it was the center of life for the middle-class people who lived nearby. With retail shops, a beauty salon, a restaurant, and one of the first movie theaters, it was the hub of activity. The Texas Theatre showed black and white movies to customers for only $.09 and was filled on Saturday mornings. Across the street was the old Safeway Grocery Store. Down one street was the milk plant, the A&W Drive-In, and one of the best cafeterias in all of Waco. Down the other street was the West Junior High, where neighborhood kids walked to attend school. Nice houses filled every lot. Providence Hospital was just three blocks away.

It was a "Leave It to Beaver" neighborhood, at least until the sixties, when African Americans began to move into the all-white community. With Civil Rights Laws passed that allowed anyone to live wherever they wanted, African Americans slowly moved from the other side of town into north Waco. Fearing others of different color and incomes, middle-class white people subsequently moved to the suburbs to build new and nicer homes while their former homes became rent houses. The businesses also abandoned their historical sites in search of better and safer locations away from "those people."

The shopping center flipped. The Texas Theatre became The Capri, an XXX porn theater. Two bars in the shopping center and a liquor store across the street replaced the family-centered community businesses. The grocery store first became a chemical storage building, then a convenience store with lottery tickets, cheap liquor, tobacco products, and day-old bread sold for twice its value. Twenty "one-liner" machines, a legal type of gambling without money exchange, drew customers in each day. The school burned, the milk plant was shut down, and predators on the streets became the new business class.

In 1988 the city condemned the old shopping center. The old theater floor had several inches of water on it from the leaking roof and graffiti covered the outside of the buildings. Although we had moved into the neighborhood ten years earlier while it was still open, we never drove near that corner on weekend nights. Yet during the daytime, we frequently passed the shopping center and prayed that God would give us the opportunity and courage to someday redeem it. Believing the Bible's claim that Christians are called to be the light that expels the darkness, instead of running away from it, it was four years after the building had been boarded up and "green tagged" by the inspectors that we made our move. We found the shopping center's owner and made our appeal. "Would you make us a deal on purchasing the center?" Without hesitation he responded, "No," then paused, "but I will give it to you." And just like that, Mission Waco became the owner of five empty buildings that many folks thought should have been razed.

As I mentioned before, a statement we have often used throughout the years is, "There is a real fine line between faith and stupid." With little money and only a few volunteers, we had suddenly become the landlords of a blighted edifice on one of the worst corners in Waco. While we had prayed for years for the opportunity, the courage to step out in faith for the sake of our neighborhood was now a reality. Unaware of the ramifications of our decision, we laughed at what happened and then gulped at the reality of the circumstances. We knew several people who took big risks with plenty of "God talk" surrounding it only to see many of those ventures implode in the years ahead. We did not have a business plan and there was certainly no philanthropist funding our bizarre acquisition. Yet we knew our hearts for the poor and marginalized were genuine, and we knew that God could use these hearts for others. We had a deep biblical theology of Christian community development that God "would rebuild the ancient ruins and restore the places long devastated; they will renew the ruined cities that have been devastated for generations" (Isa 61:4). Like Nehemiah, we were willing to become the "repairer of broken walls and restorer of streets with dwellings" (Isa 58:12), even through tears as he saw the brokenness of his own community. It was worth the risk of looking "stupid" for the sake of others. Oftentimes we had prayed the Lord's Prayer that God's kingdom would come on earth as it is in heaven, that we would not just wait for the reward of a better life after we died. Only if we put our collective faith in "being sure of what we hope for and certain of what we do not see" could God show his power and resources to our community (Heb 11:1). We confessed our weak faith but then moved onward in confidence that God could supply our every need. It was time to bring out the gloves and shovels.

George W. Bush Shows Up

Even before we could begin the initial cleanup of the old theater, a call came from the Texas Governor's Office, asking if the Governor could do a public announcement at the site. "Are you sure?" I asked. "Do you know what that building has been and how much disrepair it involves?" "Yes, we do," the representative said. "Governor Bush would like to use your site to announce his intentions of engaging ministries and organizations like Mission Waco in our nation's challenges. He is about to announce his candidacy for President of the United States and wants the nation to know his plan to include faith-based groups to do the kind of great work you are doing. In fact, if elected President, groups like yours will be able to access federal funds to support these kinds of projects."

The next day the Waco Police Department and the McLennan County Sheriff's Office, along with the Texas Highway Department, showed up early to block the streets around the old shopping center and assure safety to the dignitaries who were on the way. The whole neighborhood was buzzing as they tried to determine what was happening. As they continued to line up behind the barricades, the black limousines were escorted through the barriers and out stepped the governor, his wife, and his entourage. After a few handshakes with our staff he stepped up to the microphone and made his announcement as the national media snapped their pictures. A few minutes later they were back in the limos, headed back to the State Capitol. And while we never received any funds, Laura Bush did return to our children's program to meet and play with the neighborhood kids.

In the days ahead, the area residents began to talk to each other about the "white people" who were working on the old shopping center. There were several rumors about who we were and why we were in "their" neighborhood. As some began to personally inquire, we could only say then that we were Christians trying to bring healing and hope back to the area. "Can I help?" some would say. "Of course, grab a shovel and help us clear the debris." Another would say, "Can you hire me? I am unemployed." Since we had little money, we could only hire a few for day labor, but we did what we could. Some worked for pay then stayed on as volunteers when the money ran out, which happened frequently. Even the drug dealers and girls trapped in the web of prostitution would occasionally help with the remodeling project.

It took years, but over time the old buildings were gutted, new roofs were installed, and fresh paint, as if covering a multitude of past sins, replaced the dirt and grime. A few contractors fixed doors, installed new glass windows, unstopped sewer lines, and laid tile. When the money ran out, we waited until another source emerged. City inspectors became encouragers instead of feared guardians of the codes. They had watched the blight encroach over time and were thrilled to see positive change happen. While we still had to meet standards, there was grace that accompanied the process. One by one the green tags were removed as the goals were met, followed by celebration.

Within two years Mission Waco opened the children's center in one of the buildings. No longer limited by the front yard and basketball court at our home, children could now come to the newly renovated facility for after-school tutoring, Bible stories, activities, and refreshments. College students ventured across town to help.

The middle section of the shopping center was converted into offices and a bill-paying center. A computer lab opened in the end unit to fill the "digital-divide" that had deepened for the poor, who had virtually no technological skills. We continued our small job training program that had been created to help the unemployed solidify pre-employment work maturity skills and find jobs in the community. Area teens were also included, knowing that the best way to overcome lifetime poverty would be permanent employment. The old, abandoned bar next door was purchased to provide increased space for the growing children and youth programs. After its renovation, there were additional activities, field trips, and summer camps available for the youth, often led by volunteers and students from Baylor University and McLennan Community College. A step-dance team was formed and they began to be invited to perform at area events. The corner was abuzz with life.

In the middle section of the shopping center that was once the old porn theater was obviously a challenge to overcome—not only socially, but physically. The chairs were rotted, the walls had crumbled in several places, and the smell of mildew remained for years. A local church that was renovating their worship center called one day to offer us two hundred of their theater chairs, still in good condition. Knowing that first-run movies would not be an option, a full stage was built so it could accommodate live theater performances, dance, music, meetings, and more. Even a twenty-eight-feet-high climbing wall was built on the back wall for groups to use. Curtains were installed both on the stage and over the ugly walls, lighting and sound were added, and the old lobby that had displayed half-naked women to lure a sordid array of customers was painted in bright and beautiful colors. With only volunteers the early theater activities were average at best, but at least the purpose of the place had been redeemed.

Stevie Walker-Webb Also Shows Up

Not far from the corner, a young African American kid, who knew poverty firsthand, began attending our youth program. He was a talented and fun student who joined the step-dance team and participated in various activities including the theater. Each year his talent and leadership skills matured and his dreams took shape. In his senior year of high school, Stevie asked if we could help him go to college. Because of the generosity of a wealthy donor years before, Mission Waco was able to offer him a scholarship in addition to his Pell Grant so that he could attend The University of North Texas. It was there that his love for theater expanded and he became an esteemed student, known for his passion for using performing arts as a platform for social justice. At the end of his college experience with a dual degree in Sociology and Fine Arts, Stevie called to ask if there was any way he could get more scholarships to receive a Master of Fine Arts (MFA) at another university. Since our "Wellspring Scholarship" fund could not yet support master's level education, I offered him an alternative path. "Come back to Waco and be our first director of the Jubilee Theatre."

In the next three years, Mission Waco's community theater exploded with activities and excitement. Our new, twenty-three-year-old director had filled the seats with people of all races and economic statuses. Stevie Walker-Webb had written and directed three of his own plays, taught low-income African Americans who had never acted or performed, held successful theater camps for children throughout Waco, and secured rights to Broadway stage plays that were performed right there in the old shopping center. Many of his performances included plays that dealt with social justice. At the conclusion of several of these plays, the audiences would engage in riveting discussions about race relationships, mental health, religious hypocrisy, and homelessness. The arts page of the local newspaper celebrated this new director and the multi-cultural theater that had attracted the whole community.

Three years later the phone rang again. "You won't believe this," Stevie exclaimed. "I just heard from the best drama school in the nation that of the twelve hundred applicants for the three scholarships they offered in their acclaimed MFA program, I was chosen as one of them! I'm going to New York City!"

Mission Waco broke the glass ceiling that day. A neighborhood kid, just a few blocks away from the former porn theater, had been liberated from the bondage of poverty and racism and seen for who he really was, a talented kid filled with God's love and his own dreams, now with the opportunity to use his gifts and talents to their fullest. Today Stevie Walker-Webb has a Master of Fine Arts, directs off-Broadway plays, and helps urban children on the side.

The World Cup Café

When the neighborhood changed, almost no one from the wealthier community would even drive through the area. Economic development in the "bad part of town" was not even discussed by city leaders and local businessmen and women. Like many blighted areas in urban centers, the only income that came into the area was from drug money, payday lending, or convenience stores with overpriced items. Economic development is a key component of healing and restoring poor neighborhoods, but seminaries rarely train ministry students to learn these kinds of skills.

Mission Waco's board of directors and staff shared a deep compassion for the city's poor and marginalized and knew that genuine change would require healthy economic development over a long period of time. As we learned more about the ways Christian community developers around the nation had addressed this common issue, there were still few successful options. Inevitably, we discovered, any business investment would take us years to breakeven on and have impact. Yet with the same small, mustard seed faith that got us to this point, as well as a commitment to stay in the neighborhood for the long haul, our leadership was able to rise above the naysayers. When our last remaining building in the shopping center was rejected by numerous franchisers, even with the lure of free rent for a year, Mission Waco decided to be entrepreneurs. Knowing most restaurants are boarded up before they ever make a profit, the decision was risky at best, maybe even another "stupid" choice. We knew we would lose money for a while, but since we were a nonprofit ministry and our primary goal was getting those wealthier residents back to spend money in the area, we pursued it nonetheless.

On Valentine's Day of 2006, the World Cup Café and Fair-Trade Market were opened. The little café, located in the corner unit of the shopping center, had been renovated with bright paint, used tables and chairs, and an expensive coffee machine. A chef and wait staff were hired, and the menus were printed. Then we waited. A few customers showed up now and then, mostly friends willing to support our effort. Either from kindness or sincerity, they said they liked the food. Yet as the weeks went by, there were fewer customers and fewer dollars to verify their claims. As the bills outweighed the income, each board meeting drew more intense scrutiny. Everyone seemed to have an opinion. "We should pass out flyers. The hamburgers need more salt. Our prices are too high. Our prices are too low. Maybe we should spend that wasted money on the children's program instead of throwing it down the drain."

The board eventually agreed on an amount they were willing to lose each month, as long as the profits showed increase. Little by little the World Cup Café began to move upwards with some occasional setbacks. One of the most significant additions was the Fair-Trade Market area in the back room offering retail goods made by the world's poor. Slowly the customer profiles began to change. There were a few more white and brown customers among the mostly black ones from the neighborhood. Some of the downtown merchants wandered over to try breakfast and the daily specials. By the third year our primary goal was successful. Many of those who had grown up in the old neighborhood years ago but moved away came back to eat and talk about their old homes down the street and their good memories of the area.

After twelve years the World Cup Café made its first quarterly profit. Over the years the little restaurant has become a few times the number one breakfast place on social media. Word has spread of the café's good food and great atmosphere. It has become a fun place to eat with a deeper purpose than making money. The expanded Fair-Trade Market in the rear of the café added room for large groups. Then the mayor showed up, as well as the President of the Chamber of Commerce. The immediate neighborhood still came and diversity was consistent. The café even won some local awards through community-wide ballots. In just a few more years, we became the "best breakfast in town," according to Trip Advisor and Yelp.

Even Mark Zuckerberg and David Brooks Show Up

One of the unexpected things that happens when ministry is an open book for all to read is the surprises that come. While the World Cup Café has had thousands of diverse customers throughout the years, most have been locals, with a fair number of visitors from other cities. But occasionally we get a special customer.

"Can we use your café for a special meeting?" was the question posed to me early one week from an old friend. "Sure!" I said. "What's the occasion?" "I can't tell you," he responded, "just trust me." On the requested afternoon later that week, when the daily customers had finished their lunches, a group of twenty-five pastors began to walk through the doors of the World Cup Café for the secret meeting with an unknown guest. A few minutes later Mark Zuckerberg, the world's fifth wealthiest man, walked through the door. After a few welcoming handshakes, we sat down for a one-hour conversation with the A.D.O and Founder of Facebook, at his request, as he toured cities across America to listen to their concerns. He exited nearly as soon as he had entered. By the next morning, the local newspaper and social media had exploded with hits about the World Cup Café and our famous customer who only drank water that day.

But the next well-known customer did eat breakfast. David
Brooks is a conservative political columnist for the *Washington
Post* and *New York Times*, as well as a PBS television commen-
tator. I had been invited by Brooks and his wife, Anne Snyder,
to Washington, D.C. earlier in the year to participate in a three-
day retreat for some three hundred and fifty "Weavers," who
were doing local neighborhood work among the poor and marginalized. Brooks and Snyder had come to believe that groups
around the nation like Mission Waco were the best answer to
our national challenges. Having become somewhat cynical with
a political system that rarely seemed to impact significant issues, the couple responded to my request to come to Waco for
a community forum we hosted. The day before the gathering,
Brooks met me on "our corner" to eat at the World Cup Café
and see the renovated theater, nonprofit Jubilee Food Market,
Urban REAP aquaponics greenhouse, and liquor-store-turned
-economic-development-center. One of his breakfast guests was
a local community leader whose family had been instrumen-
tal in enacting change for over four decades, especially among
lower-income African Americans.

The Gift of Listening

Brooks and Zuckerberg were engaging national figures who
brought encouragement to our community. While opinions
vary widely about the Facebook founder, Zuckerberg was here,
in our local community, listening to others about their views on
how change is happening in smaller communities. He and his
wife were traveling the nation, often in towns much smaller than
Waco, to listen. I was fascinated that he really did that with our
group. Rarely, it seems, do national politicians really listen to
the concerns of local neighborhoods, much less seek to address
those concerns. As a wealthy businessman, he received no votes
for attending. In fact, since the majority in our meeting were
local pastors and he is not a Christian, it surprised me when he
asked about Church Under the Bridge and some of the other
work of pastors who were tutoring children in low-performing

schools. Zuckerberg was born into a Jewish family but became an agnostic as an adult. Since he and his wife had children, they were now listening to other views of faith as seekers.

David Brooks' story is even more fascinating. As a prolific writer, much of his own story, told in his book *The Second Mountain: The Quest for a Moral Life*, is about his personal journey of divorce, family estrangement and despair, then faith in Christ, remarriage, and engagement with local kids in D.C. After years of seeking the world's ideas of success, Brooks reordered his values while seeking the "Second Mountain." His new faith had ignited a desire to make a difference in local communities. Since then, Brooks has helped create a national organization known as "Weave, The Social Fabric Project," calling people to "quietly work across America to end loneliness and isolation and weave inclusive communities and shifting our culture from hyper-individualism that is all about personal success, to relationalism that puts relationships at the center of our lives" (The Aspen Institute 2020).

In the Food Desert

Most Americans tend to think that hunger is primarily due to a lack of financial resources to buy food. Although that reality is part of the issue, physical access to healthy and affordable food has become the nation's biggest challenge. One in every seven U.S. households (14.3 percent) are "food insecure." They spend 30 percent more money for food than their wealthier counterparts. The U.S. Department of Agriculture's Economic Research Service estimates 25.3 million people live in what we also call "food deserts," far removed from grocery stores. One half of them are low income residents with little access to transportation. The USDA defines a food desert as a "low-access community" with at least five hundred people and/or at least 33 percent of the census tract's population residing more than one mile from a supermarket or large grocery store. For rural census tracts this distance is more than ten miles. Convenience stores, commonly found in food deserts, sell overpriced, processed, and fat-laden

foods, with few vegetables and fruits, adding to the health issues
of poorer neighborhoods.

Our neighbors knew we cared about them mentally, physically, and spiritually. As the area began to become better, many
of the residents appealed to our staff for help finding access to
healthier and affordable food. The closest full grocery store was
a little over two miles away. Walking almost five miles round
trip or taking the inefficient bus system that took almost as
long and cost $3 round trip were little incentive to make the
journey worthwhile.

Across the street from the World Cup Café was the
6500-square-feet, predatory convenience store which once had
been a Safeway Grocery Store where the neighbors shopped. But
as the numbers of the poor increased in north Waco and super-
markets began to relocate in higher traffic and wealthier areas,
the grocery store closed. In its place was A.J.'s Market. The store
sold no fruits or vegetables, only canned items with little taste
and lots of salt and calories. "Please help us get a real grocery
store," our friends begged.

For over four years, Mission Waco bartered with the owners
to sell us the old building for a reasonable price. Even though
the renters had been cited for food stamp fraud, they reopened
under another name and continued to hold firm to purchase
prices over three times the tax appraisal rate. Years went by and
we waited. Then one stormy night, the roof on the convenience
store tore open and rain covered the floor. It was a horrible
mess, horrible enough that we received a long-awaited phone
call offering to sell us the old building for a reasonable price.
The deal was made and Mission Waco became the proud owners of yet another old building, filled with a bad roof and a long
list of other problems.

We later discovered that before the closing was completed,
thieves had broken into the building and ripped out all the copper wiring and metal for resale, which would eventually cost us
thousands more in repairs. The new roof was also costly, but

there was little choice. We wondered, "Was this a full-scale 'stupid' decision or could God redeem it, too?"

A neighborhood meeting was called to seek community input and affirm again our purpose in the area. Our staff had gone door to door throughout the area to be sure everyone knew about the meeting. About sixty-five neighbors showed up to look around the facility, meet and greet each other, and make suggestions for the best use of the space. Twelve ideas were copied down on the white board for everyone to see. Then the voting began. Within a few minutes it was obvious by a strong 75 percent lead that the neighbors wanted a grocery store with healthy and affordable food. To make sure they understood the implications of their choice, our leaders informed those who attended that the risk was high, since grocery stores make little profit on food, the cost to renovate the building would be steep, and Mission Waco would not sell liquor, tobacco products, or lottery tickets. With that said we shared refreshments and enjoyed more personal conversations.

Within a few weeks of the purchase, I began to fret about the reality of the Jubilee Food Market ever coming into existence. I did not want to disappoint our neighbors, but the more I asked and looked for a solid business plan, the more I worried. The following week I was speaking in a large church in Dallas, and shared the news of our recent purchase and my fears. At the end of the talk, two men approached me and introduced themselves. Nick said, "I supervised a large chain of grocery stores for forty years and recently retired." Mark said, "I build those same stores all over the Metroplex." Both said, "We can help you!"

Not only did these two men drive one hundred miles to Waco the next week, but they contacted another Christian who builds and installs grocery store refrigeration and shelving. The next meeting now included a retail manager who was only months from retirement, an architect who helped design Mission Waco's homeless shelter and café, a construction contractor, and two others that wanted to hear more about this crazy idea of defying the odds. The group of ten agreed to meet every two weeks for several hours to determine the feasibility of the project, including the estimated cost of remodeling, filling the building with groceries, and hiring and training staff. The Dream Team was an incredible group of men who loved God, cared for the poor, and had vocational skills that were critical for the project.

Within a few months, we realized we would need at least $650,000 to open the doors. In fact, it was more. The final cost was $925,000. Since Mission Waco's existing program budget required significant financial support unrelated to this huge project, the odds seemed stacked against us. Waco's poverty rate, 28.7 percent, was already double most cities. And even if by some miracle we could complete the project, the likelihood of making enough income selling food in a poor community seemed remote.

In November of 2016, the Jubilee Food Market doors swung open to the huge crowd of well-wishers and neighbors in the parking lot. The grand opening included neighborhood children singing, words of appreciation to our team, honorary praise to donors and contractors, a ribbon cutting, and free pizza and Dr. Pepper for all. The Dream Team stood back and soaked it all in. God had used their talents to make a high impact project a reality—all for the kingdom of God.

A few years have passed since that ceremony, but the celebration goes on. The business plan is exceeding its projection to break even within five years. Neighbors continue to shop and thank the staff for healthy and affordable food. The wider community shops there too, a necessary part of the success. Loyalty cards were created to reward cash back to those living within one mile of the store. Health surveys have been taken, tasty food preparation has been taught by local chefs, and ethnic foods have been added.

Interested city leaders from Dallas, Houston, and Austin have all visited the store to explore the concept and feasibility for them to address similar issues in their own food deserts. Students and volunteers have come to consider the potential of the model in their context. Most of our visitors are fascinated that all this effort emerged from a Christian nonprofit organization which genuinely cared for the poor, engaging the passion and talents of hundreds of volunteers and donors who partnered and invested in the neighborhood. Unlike quick-fix strategies, Christian community development has offered a substantive and lasting alternative that engages the neighborhood and provides dignity.

In the Liquor Store

Economic development continued to be an important priority for change. While most models of community change are built around wealthy business folks giving money to nonprofits that work with the poor, those same business leaders have unique gifts that all cities need. It is not making money that is the sin of the wealthy, it is what they do with those resources that shapes their hearts. Healthy neighborhoods need thriving merchants to offer basic goods and services for their residents. Business leaders, especially Christian ones, can help address the economic blight in their own communities like few others.

The last icon of the deterioration of this north Waco neighborhood was an old liquor store. For thirty years Martha Jane's Package Store had been the closest location for every kind of liquor—yet it had also become a growing site for unsavory customers. Several years after Mission Waco had worked so hard to dispel the negative image of the north Waco neighborhood, a man walked into Martha Jane's store, picked up a bottle of Jack Daniel's, then hit her across the head. He quickly stole money from the cash register and ran. Martha Jane fell to the ground and had to be taken to the hospital. The nightly television news ran the story with full video replay of the crime, while the police continued to look for the robber. All our work to create a new image of the area was undone. Once again we were stigmatized as the bad part of town.

In the summer of 2017, God convicted a Christian businessman from Dallas, who was a friend of Mission Waco, to donate the money to purchase the old liquor store and its adjoining building as a small economic center for the neighborhood. As a wealthy businessman who believed in the holistic gospel, he recognized his unique role in rebuilding, restoring, and renewing communities long devastated as part of the kingdom of God, just as the prophet Isaiah talks about. Like many financially successful Christians who really want their whole communities to prosper, they grow weary of funding more church buildings and instead look for investments that impact urban neighborhoods. They recognize that the gospel becomes more credible when the "least of these" are impacted by their donations.

As with the Jubilee Food Market and any good community development project, Mission Waco hosted a listening party with all the neighbors to explore what kinds of goods and services were needed in the neighborhood. Twenty-four ideas were suggested by over fifty stakeholders that day. While some of them were unreasonable, the neighbors wanted a beauty shop, a small library, a laundromat, a "dollar store," a small clothing store, and even a pizza restaurant, since most of the pizza franchises would not deliver in the area. They wanted what most of the community wanted or had, but in their own neighborhood.

In June of 2019, the first unit of "The Colcord Center" was completed. A few interested businesses had contacted our volunteer real estate broker, who happened to also be our City Council representative who fought hard for our lower-income area. One of those businesses was the perfect fit. A young Hispanic businessman was insistent on putting his family's second Mexican ice cream and sweets shop in the shiny new vacancy. Not only did he fit our preference as a minority business owner, he also had business experience and success in his first store. After a couple of months personalizing the building, Helados La Aztecas opened their doors to a huge crowd of customers and neighbors. They have had lines at their counter ever since then to buy items like mangonadas, sandia rebanaditas, horchata ice cream, chamoy, and more. With our growing Hispanic population, about 70 percent of the customers are from our surrounding neighborhoods.

Two adjacent units are currently being remodeled. This portion of the 1930s building had been vacated decades before and no longer had a roof. To meet Waco's building design standards and codes has meant a long process of input from an architect, engineer, and several inspectors. Our desire to save the original exterior to maintain the look has meant additional steel support, which has led to even more fundraising. But as the walls are going up, the phones are already ringing with people requesting details for potential occupancy. While many Christians wonder what rehabbing a liquor store into a business center has to do with faith, we have physical, social, and economic evidence that validates the promise of Isaiah 58:12: "Your people will rebuild the ancient ruins and will raise up the age-old foundations; you will be called Repairer of Broken Walls, Restorer of Streets with Dwellings."

It is harder to raise money for an economic center than for a grocery store. Most donors like the feeling of meeting a basic human need. Our efforts to provide shoes for the homeless, coats for the poor, school supplies and Christmas toys for the lower-income children, or even camp scholarships for our urban teens are significantly easier to raise since these donations bring immediate satisfaction to the giver. Finding resources for job training, alcohol and drug recovery, mental health counseling, and a "free clinic" are much more challenging. To support the renovation of an economic center certainly does not engender the warm fuzzy feelings like the others. Yet any city planner knows that breaking the cycle of blighted communities requires economic development as well as community development. Recapturing money streams that once invigorated older neighborhoods, but later ended up in the hands of more affluent areas, brings vitality back. Studies show that if both low-income and middle-class shoppers occasionally invest in retail stores, restaurants, and services in under-resourced neighborhoods, the impact significantly changes the area. Jobs for neighbors, community pride, beautification efforts, and the synergy needed to attract other stores and offices to the area multiply.

Unfortunately, philanthropists, developers, and city leaders often refuse to invest in challenged areas, preferring to put their dollars into areas of the city that already experience levels of success. Business leaders want "a return for their money," and reducing risk is part of their formula. Challenging that circular thinking is part of the job of Christian community developers. Advocating for economic change to city councils, foundations, and venture capitalists requires a long and relentless effort, using all kinds of strategies. Helping Christians reconsider their next fundraising drive for another "feel-good project" in order to invest in rebuilding broken systemic issues of neighborhoods is difficult, even though it can reap enormous benefits in communities over time. Yet few churches and Christian businessmen and women have chosen this path. Most of the wealth in churches and communities is rarely invested in strategies which ultimately empower the poor and marginalized of their own cities.

In Decaying Houses

Finding affordable housing in the old neighborhood was a huge challenge. Former residents who had moved to the suburbs heard of Mission Waco's community development work and offered great deals or donations of their decaying homes or vacant lots. Although Habitat for Humanity eventually built fifty homes for low-income qualifiers in the neighborhood, the need for quality housing exceeded their model. Fortunately, as in most communities, there were successful real estate developers who were Christians willing to use their unique skills to help Mission Waco address this need. These professionals were gathered together to explore the challenges and opportunities in the area. Vacant lots were cheap and relatively easy to acquire. Demolition of some of the donated houses took more time and volunteers. Getting banks to lend credit for new homes in the area was challenging, especially to area renters who had little credit and significant debt. With influence and wisdom, the new volunteer team went to work, eventually creating a separate nonprofit housing ministry and hiring a director to work alongside Mission Waco.

Through the years Grassroots Development Corporation overcame those major hurdles and built over sixty new homes in the area. While most of the original houses were purchased by lower-income folks with jobs who completed credit repair classes, middle-income housing emerged too. Driven by a growing number of younger, college-educated adults, the new residents decided they preferred to live in the diverse, older area of Waco instead of the monoculture of the suburbs. With over 125 new and remodeled mixed-income houses, there was a growing sense of change emerging.

To Our Unsustainable World

Perhaps the most unusual building project came through a grant written to an energy company's nonprofit foundation. Since the poor throughout the world experience the worst results of environmental inequities, we needed to find a way to help awaken wealthy, wasteful, and apathetic people to the ecological crisis at hand. Lack of clean water, poor soil quality, homes with lead-based paint, air pollution, climate changes, acid rain, deforestation, litter, and other increasingly toxic factors are reducing the quality of life for billions of our local and global inhabitants.

Seeking an educational model to teach creation care, a carefully crafted proposal was written to Green Mountain Energy's Sun Club Foundation requesting funds for an urban project that would teach the importance of addressing the growing environmental crisis. Sustainability and care of God's "very good" earth was given as a cultural mandate by the Creator God in Genesis 1:28: "Be fruitful and multiply and increase in number; fill the earth and subdue it." He gave them every seed-bearing plant for food, with the reminder that he would supply basic needs for them as they honored the basic principles of caring for the environment.

Not only did Mission Waco Mission World receive the initial grant to build an aquaponics greenhouse in the middle of our slowly recovering neighborhood, but the Sun Club Foundation invited us to ask for additional funds to multiply the teaching components. With the help of four professors from two universities and an architect, solar panels, a rainwater catchment system, and an amazing composter that turns household waste items into high quality compost in just twenty-four hours was added to the proposal. The entire system, called Urban REAP (Renewable Energy and Agricultural Project), was funded and constructed the following year. Today hundreds of children, youth, and adults from all over the nation have experienced our tour and learned about how each one of them can be a better steward of God's creation and impact the limited resources for the environment. From purchasing organic leafy greens, fish, compost, or flowers, most visitors become more committed to the significant practices they can do to address the pollution and harmful lifestyles affecting our world.

The same philosophy of ministry has led Mission Waco Mission World to do Christian community development in various parts of the world where poverty is even more overwhelming. The ministry has provided hundreds of water wells, microloans, and school sponsorships in northeast Haiti for twenty-seven years. We have helped poor tribes in north India with healthcare access. Alongside this we have engaged in projects with the homeless orphans in Mexico City, some mentally and physically disabled. All are driven by a holistic understanding of Christian ministry that sees beyond geographic borders and nationalism. "The earth is the LORD's, and everything in it, the world, and all who live in it" (Ps 24:1).

Repairers of Broken Churches

For the last twenty-five years, Janet and I have worked with the homeless and poor. I still pastor a local church of almost three hundred members that began with five homeless men and women meeting under an interstate bridge where they lived. Most of them were struggling with addiction of some sort and some form of mental illness. Church Under the Bridge began after my wife and I invited them to join us across the street at a local restaurant for breakfast in 1992. Since neither of us understood the real issues of homelessness, we implored about the reasons they now lived under a bridge. The conversation accelerated into deeply painful stories of their pasts and family life. Some of the homeless had been abused as children, rejected by peers, divorced, disabled, unemployed, and marginalized. Schizophrenia, PTSD, bipolar disorder, and chronic depression had impacted several of them. Crack cocaine, "40 ouncers," and other drugs became the natural medications to ease the pain and loneliness. With comorbidity, these dually diagnosed men and women had become chronically homeless, many for decades. With a backpack and sleeping bag, the "losers" of the culture found other broken friends and acquaintances who become a type of family.

After three weeks of breakfasts, my bill had risen to $250 with the growing attendees. Since a bond of sorts had developed, the homeless customers recognized our financial challenge and suggested that Janet and I come over to their home under the interstate bridge and lead a Bible study. The next Sunday morning a small circle of chairs was arranged beneath the noise of 18-wheelers passing overhead. Janet led a few songs and I led a short Bible study from Romans. The conversation that followed was very engaging, with numerous opinions and questions. Unlike the boredom of so many church services, that morning was unlike any other I had ever experienced.

When church ended, the small group invited us back for the following Sunday. We returned. A few more homeless folks showed up that second Sunday, including one man who had been standing on the busy corner holding his newly written cardboard sign, "Come to Bible study!" Each week they came, often ready with new questions about God, Jesus, the Bible, other religions, ethical dilemmas, losing salvation, hell, and why God lets bad things happen. It was so fun to be in real conversations with people that were genuinely searching and asking. And they loved to sing, even though few could carry a tune.

In the weeks and months that followed, my life became complicated by this church. I received phone calls from the county jail from some in our group that had gotten drunk and arrested for fighting in those late nights under the bridge. "Can you bail me out, bro?" Other requests followed. "Can you give me a ride to the emergency room?" "Can I borrow a couple of bucks?" "Know anybody that I could do some yardwork for?" Without experience among the homeless and poor, I didn't know how to answer and realized over time how many ignorant choices I made that enabled them. Even so, we never questioned our friendship with these disenfranchised men and women who knew we cared. I had found a new sense of joy in a ragtag church of the broken that I never experienced in the world of the middle class.

There were some other challenges that pushed our deepening call to reconsider these complicated relationships. On more than one occasion, some of them would urinate or defecate on themselves during a physical seizure or intoxicated stupor. Trying hard not to embarrass them, we cleaned up their messes, tolerated their body odor, washed filthy clothing, and bought a lot of clean underwear. No one in our discipleship classes had ever prepared us for this lesson.

The irony of our little "flock" is that it caused us to discover church for the first time. It was unorthodox and challenging, yet somehow very genuine. Broken people who know they are messed up often have humble hearts beneath the outward façade. They often believe they are worthless and unlovable, society reminding them of this regularly. With awkward social skills, bad habits, and unproductive lifestyles, many in our little church were much quicker to talk about life and share their sins than many of the church members down the street in the "real church." In his book, called *Hard Living People & Mainstream Christians*, Tex Sample shares lessons learned from his seminary students who he sent out to interview the "hard-living" folks of the city. Sample even includes the expletives and sordid stories of the lives of a vast array of prostitutes, street beggars, homeless, drug dealers, alcoholics, and low-income workers who, surprising for some, had a high view of God, yet a low view of the clergy. They did not like all the hymns but loved loud country music that shared songs of divorce, pain, and loneliness. They could relate to Jesus, since he "had no place to lay his head," was harassed by the "religious people," and was willing to touch the lepers, heal the sick, and confront the hypocrites.

Like Sample, we found that many of those under the bridge wanted more than a handout. They wanted relationships with others who would love them as they were. We discovered that an afternoon softball game or fishing trip meant more than another coat dropped off at the intersection where some of our church members panhandled. They played the game of the "do-gooder Christians" who dropped off Bibles, religious tracts, and food with "Jesus loves you" marked across it. Many "got saved" several times a week, since that was the expected outcome of donors who stopped to talk.

Through the first twenty-six years, Church Under the Bridge never left the interstate underpass. As the crowd of worshipers grew to include others, we added porta potties, a flatbed trailer for a stage, more chairs, and a sound system that could compete with the noise of overhead trucks. What began as a few homeless folks talking in a circle became a worship service with music, testimonies, and thoughtful Bible devotions, frequently from the homeless people themselves. Food was provided each week. A mentally ill man who wanted to "lead worship" was given an electric guitar, just never plugged in. Students from the university began to show up along with unchurched middle-class attendees of all races. We offered communion, baptism, and even hosted weddings and funerals. Some of the addicted found alcohol and drug treatment, others got jobs. While some of those harder to reach stood at the back and talked, many moved to the chairs over time. There was freedom to come and go, with little emphasis on giving money, since many of them had left churches who constantly did their own begging.

Dignity is paramount for us "trolls" at Church Under the Bridge. Paternalism is not. Everyone matters, everyone has a story, everyone has a name. We celebrate victories, no matter how small they are to the bigger world.

After twenty-six years under the interstate, the Texas Highway Department of Transportation contacted me to say we would have to move Church Under the Bridge, since the State had finally allocated $340 million to tear down and reconstruct the aging bridges along with 0.6 miles of interstate over the next three years. The local newspaper ran a story entitled "Homeless Church About to Be Homeless." With a congregation that had grown to 250 or more, we began to look for options. Within a couple of weeks, a surprising call came. "Chip and Joanna Gaines would like to invite your church to use the Magnolia Silos courtyard on Sundays for your church since we are not open then." A few weeks later, our unconventional church and a local middle school band marched from the bridge to the Silos, singing "O When the Saints Go Marching In." What had become the pilgrimage site for thirty thousand shoppers each week to Waco became our temporary home while the bridges are demolished and reconstruction started. We make a habit of thanking taxpaying Texans for their generosity in funding our new $340 million "church building" that will cost us nothing.

Though Janet and I have been blessed with a lifetime of Christian discipleship, church programs, and theological training, we agree that God has stretched and deepened our faith more in our time with the unchurched rather than the churched. In my book, *Trolls and Truth*, I share the real stories of fourteen of our "church friends" who have taught me more about God, faith, and the church than any previous experiences or training. In many ways we live in two worlds, often having to explain them to one another. I have also come to appreciate the prophetic lifestyle of Jesus, who sat with a prostitute, touched lepers, turned over tables at the synagogue, and called out the outwardly religious Pharisees who had missed the very essence of God's kingdom. I have moved from fruitless anger at the modern American church to sadness for it, especially as the Western culture is walking away from church completely. We need "new wineskins" where rich and poor are the church together, learning from each other about the God of all (Matt 9:14). I have reached a place of healthy anticipation for what God is still doing to prepare the "bride of Christ" to be ready.

5

THE BIBLE IS NOT A CHILDREN'S BOOK

"God helps those who help themselves," said a U.S. Congressman in a small group meeting we had with him. As a respected leader and church-going Christian, I didn't have the courage to tell him in front of the others that his stated Bible verse is not even in the Bible. His main point—that poor people need to do something themselves to alleviate their poverty—rings true in some ways. While he was correct at some level, such a simplistic statement does not acknowledge the larger issue that there is a "blame the poor" middle-class mentality. Both the Bible and research have much more to say about the poor and poverty than his dismissive words.

Reading the Bible and understanding the Bible are often terms used interchangeably. Naturally, many Christians without the use of basic interpretation skills simply read the words through the lenses of their own cultural background. For example, the following verse is often misinterpreted by contemporary Christians whose view is that there is little they can do with such a big issue of poverty, and even Jesus knew it. Not so!

"The poor will always be with you," Jesus said that day at the table as he ate with his disciples (John 12:8; Matt 26:1; Mark 14:7). What he meant and how we interpret it is often taken out of context. On the surface it seems as if this task of helping the poor is an unending effort we will never win. What successful

American wants to be part of a losing battle? There are so many poor people in our world. In the face of so much work one's impulse is often, "Quit wasting your time. Your efforts won't amount to anything."

But the verse has a second half that adds clarity to Jesus' real message. The entire verse says, "The poor you will always have with you, but you will not always have me." Jesus is telling Judas and the other disciples to leave Mary alone as he commends her for her humble and generous act of washing his feet with an expensive jar of perfume. Since he would soon be gone from the world, her act of reverence was especially timely. There would be time to help the poor again; it was a basic biblical norm of ongoing discipleship. The Bible clearly says that Christians are expected to help the poor. Even though the poor will always be here, we do have work to do on their behalf, regardless of the overwhelming challenges.

Jesus was also quoting Deuteronomy, which says, "If among you, one of your brothers should become poor, in any of your towns within your land that the Lord your God is giving you, you shall not harden your heart or shut your hand against your poor brother, but you shall open your hand to him and lend him sufficient for his need, whatever it may be . . . For the poor you will always have with you in the land. Therefore, I command you, 'You shall open wide your hand to your brother, to the needy and to the poor, in your land'" (Deut 15:7-11).

Unfortunately, many Christians misuse the Bible to justify their own agendas. While it may or may not be true that ending global poverty will never be complete, especially when unrepentant sinners rule the earth, today millions are still living because of the efforts of compassionate men and women who are choosing to make a difference. John's Gospel assures us that Judas did not want to sell Mary's expensive bottle of perfume and give the money to the poor. The gospel reveals Judas' self-centeredness and deceit, for Judas alone carried the money bag of the disciples, and his heart and actions were unscrupulous.

Not only do selfish motives warp biblical views, cultural conditions do so as well. In biblical times, particularly in the Old Testament, wealth was often considered to be a blessing or a sign of God's approval. Abraham was wealthy, as were others. This chosen leader of God's people had earned his privilege and wealth and was an example to men in Israel. Naturally, the rich young ruler, a good and ethical Jew who prided himself as a keeper of the commandments since boyhood, assumed his own wealth and respect as an upstanding religious man was deserved. Many of the wealthy today still view their privilege as deserved for "being good" and "being religious." Based on that view, it becomes natural to assume that poor and marginalized people are poor because of their lack of being good and religious.

By the time of the Roman Empire, social conditions changed, as did the presupposition that wealth among the Jews was a reward. At that time, Jewish people accounted for less than 10 percent of the population. The average family lived in a one-room, two-level dwelling often shared with extended family members. Privacy was a rare commodity. Jewish families usually ate two simple meals a day, consisting mostly of bread, and often shared with friends in hours of lively conversation. The streets outside were smelly with discarded food. The Romans, however, ate four meals a day of meat and dairy. About one half of the empire's wealth was owned by only 1 to 2 percent of the elite, most of them being political, military, or religious leaders. Some 5 to 7 percent were considered rich, mostly bureaucrats. Only 15 percent were considered middle class, while 70 to 80 percent lived in poverty; these were the farmers, fishermen, herders, subsistence laborers, and slaves. Jesus' disciples were in this category.

No longer claiming a right to privilege, now the Christian community's role in the pagan Roman Empire was to challenge the greed and sensuality of the wealthy with a lifestyle built more around relationships, sharing, and care for others. Tertullian commended the Christian faith that challenged the pagan world. He gives us priceless insight into the practices of early Christian

worship, discipline, leadership selection, and financial giving.
But most significantly, Tertullian preserves the amazing pagan
observation of the Christians: "See how they love one another,"
Sociologist Rodney Stark says of the early Christians. "Christianity revitalized life in Greco-Roman cities by providing new
norms and new kinds of social relationships able to cope with
many urgent problems. To cities filled with the homeless and
impoverished, Christianity offered charity as well as hope. To
cities filled with newcomers and strangers, Christianity offered
an immediate basis for attachment. To cities filled with orphans
and widows, Christianity provided a new and expanded sense of
family. To cities torn by violent ethnic strife, Christianity offered
a new basis for social solidarity" (Stark 1996, 161).

God's Law always called for his people to protect the poor
and oppressed. In Exodus, Leviticus, and Deuteronomy, guidelines of social responsibility are given to the Israelites that are
keeping with his compassion, not one's self-righteousness. Loving God and loving one another have always coexisted together
in his kingdom. While some would become more wealthy and
powerful than others, the Law still provided guidelines to care
for the materially poor. For example, there were guidelines for
the poor to glean the fields so they could eat. Usury (interest)
was not allowed by a fellow Jew when money was borrowed. The
socially challenged, like strangers ("aliens"), were to be treated
as fellow countrymen. Widows, orphans, and slaves were to be
treated fairly and kindly as well. And all of these people were not
to be denied justice because of their class distinction.

In the Law, a person was considered poor if he only had one
coat and could not provide for the basic needs of his family
that day. Yet God's people were offered options for those who
struggled. In Exodus 22:26-27, God required that a poor person
who offered his coat in exchange for food for his family was to
get his coat back before sunset after the debt of work was paid.
Coats served as coverings in the cool evenings. Over the years
the wealthy began to take advantage of these guidelines. By
the time the eighth-century prophets arrive there are flagrant
abusers of the Law. In the book of Amos, God sends the young

prophet into the streets to address the corruption against those who are poor and oppressed. Amos 2:6-8 says, "For three sins of Israel, even for four, I will not turn back my wrath; they sell the righteous for silver, and the needy for a pair of sandals. They trample on the heads of the poor as upon dust of the ground and deny justice to the oppressed. Father and son use the same girl and so profane my holy name. They lie down beside every altar on garments taken in pledge in the house of their god. They drink wine taken as fines."

God has always cared for the poor and how his people treat them. There are more Bible verses about wealth and poverty than most all other subjects of the Bible. In the New International Version translation, the words "poor" and "poverty" appear 446 times in 384 separate verses in the Bible. The word "wealth," often translated as "greedy," can be found 1,453 times in 1,273 verses. The word "heaven" is used 662 times and the word "hell" 13 times. These counts do not include the word "justice," which is used even more frequently when addressing the poor and marginalized. Additionally, out of the thirty-one parables that Jesus tells in the Gospels, over half of them deal with the misuse of wealth, social class, debt, and wages for workers. Ignoring these Biblical words or casually reinterpreting them to fit one's own preferred explanations is dangerous.

In the Greco-Roman world, as well as in our own Western culture, social structures often support power, prestige, and privilege. "The Israelite and Jewish understanding of wealth and poverty has a different starting point" (Rhee 2012, 27). The Torah guided Israel to protect the poor and seek to keep them from poverty. The prophets and psalmists understood the poor as victims of the injustices that crush and oppress them (Amos 4:1). "He who oppresses the poor shows contempt for their Maker, but whoever is kind to the needy honors God" (Prov 14:31). This view was quite different from the elitist Romans, who described the poor as a lesser class that deserved their unfortunate status.

These are frequent themes, especially in Luke's Gospel. There are warnings about choosing worldly treasures over

God, the love of money as the root of all evil, the deceitfulness of riches, forgetting the poor, building bigger barns, and other challenging words that signify the spiritual poverty that comes to the rich. Wealth, poverty, and justice are major themes of the Scriptures. While children's stories fill the Bible, we need to be reminded that it is a book for adults with a mature worldview, called to implement God's order, rather than our culture's order, toward others.

The First Testament

The Pentateuch

The Old Covenant, including the Levitical and Deuteronomic moral guidelines, was given by God to Moses and Israel on Mount Sinai. These covenantal laws included the Ten Commandments and numerous moral, civil, criminal, and religious codes showing the newfound Israelite nation how to be a "holy nation," loving God and loving one another. First mentioned in Leviticus 25, the Year of Jubilee was introduced as a major aspect of Israelite life, highlighted as a unique economic upheaval of social injustice on the fiftieth year, following seven sabbatical years. The purpose was to remind all of Israel of their kinship and position with Yahweh, whether slave or free. On that year the social order that had become humanly corrupted by systemic injustice was to be reordered. Slaves were to be set free, debts were to be forgiven, land and people were to rest, and property was to be returned to the original owners, reminding Israel that both they and their possessions belonged to God. While scholars are unsure if the Year of Jubilee was ever enacted, the purpose was clear. It was vital in God's economy to restore relationships from the barriers of man.

Wisdom Literature
(Job, Psalms, Proverbs, Ecclesiastes, Song of Solomon)

The Proverbs frequently remind readers of the importance of relationships with the poor. "Whoever oppresses the poor shows contempt for their Maker, but whoever is kind to the needy honors God" (Prov 14:31). "Whoever is kind to the poor lends to the Lord, and he will reward them for what they have done" (Prov 19:17). "Whoever mocks the poor insults his Maker" (Prov 17:5).

The Prophets

During many summers as a child I went to Dallas to stay with my grandparents for several weeks. After a few years, my grandmother asked me to watch my grandfather more closely to be sure he did not walk away from the store and get lost, but occasionally he became disoriented, and misplaced things in the store. Even his personality began to change. What I could not understand in my young age was that my grandfather had growing dementia caused by what they called the "hardening of the arteries."

Atherosclerosis, or "plaque attack," results from hardening or narrowing of the arteries from plaque, slowing blood and oxygen to the body and ultimately leading to stroke, heart attack, or organ failure. Atherosclerosis is the number one cause of death and disability in the developed world. It is caused by high blood pressure, diabetes, smoking, or high cholesterol. A good diet, exercise, and healthy lifestyle can prevent or slow the disease, as well as certain medications. Vascular bypass surgery or angioplasty have been effective ways to reopen the blood flow and improve quality of life.

Like many physical diseases, there are spiritual dynamics and changes occurring in our lives that go unnoticed for years. Parents expect children to be selfish with their toys because it is a natural stage of development. As children become teens, parents are delighted to see signs of maturity such as sharing, politeness, and caring for others. As young adults get jobs and take on community responsibilities, those same parents swell with pride to realize their children have "grown up" in so many ways. God created this natural order that leads to healthy lives.

However, with early behavioral signs of selfishness, inappropriate attitudes, and moral failure increasing through recent years, there seems to be a spiritual crisis growing. Many parents hurt deeply as they watch their children regress and make choices that have lifetime impacts.

There are other signs that may not be as easy to observe but have equally destructive implications. As plaque slowly attaches itself to arteriolar walls, over time these more culturally acceptable sins lead to metaphorical heart issues. Pride and greed are chief among these sins. Unlike character flaws that are offensive, pride is often seen as the trait of a strong self-image and a good leader. Yet Jesus could see the pride of the religious leaders in his day. He frequently confronted their false piety and hard hearts. Once, when he healed a demon possessed man, he called them a "brood of vipers" (Matt. 12:34), recognizing that the mouth speaks from what is really inside their evil hearts. Jesus could see clearly how their twisted religion and personal pride had squelched the Spirit of God.

In C. S. Lewis' fascinating allegory, *The Great Divorce*, the bus riders bound for hell had developed a reprobate mindset, ultimately rejecting God's invitation into his presence. The final hell beyond this lifetime is the one they chose. Heaven's gates were nearby but they could not see it because of their hardened hearts. As described in Peck's chaotic stage (Peck 1998, 187–89), the depraved mindset leads to a "malignant narcissism" that becomes almost inescapable. Blasphemy is the final, distorted condition that calls God's ways evil and man's evil good.

Since the beginning of human time, the struggle between faith and possessions has existed. When Adam and Eve rebelled, their sin was rooted in greed—they wanted what they did not have. God forbade them from eating from the Tree of Knowledge of Good and Evil, with the warning that doing so would lead to death. Temptation to have what they did not led to a choice that had both physical and eternal consequences. The fruit was not just good for food, but it was "pleasing to the eye" and "desirable for gaining wisdom" (Gen 3:6).

Throughout the Old Testament, the journey of Israel to and in the Promised Land was fraught with numerous stories of greed and power. God's love was gracious and redemptive. Yet he continued to send messengers that said "his ways were not our ways" and consequences would again follow as Israel rejected his ways.

In the eighth century B.C., Israel had sunk to a new low. While Jews were attending Temple and living outwardly pious lives, there was an underbelly of greed and power like never before. The poor, consisting of farmers, common laborers, herdsmen, small merchants, artisans, and slaves, were the bulk of the population. The wealthy merchants, landowners, and professional religious leaders, though smaller in number, controlled the city infrastructure and lived in luxury. Justice and righteousness were absent. The duplicity of outward religion and the oppression of the poor seemed to incite the ire of God like never before. The covenant God had made with Israel had been forgotten and ignored. God sent several prophets into these treacherous societies to rebuke the greedy and powerful and urge them to repent, reminding them of the coming destruction if changes did not occur.

Amos, Isaiah, Hosea, and Micah were the mouthpieces of God, called to confront the social injustices of their day. They were ordinary men driven by courage, men who were willing to speak out against the greed and power of their day with warnings that no one wanted to hear. "God is sick of your pious fasting," Isaiah declares, "and wants only to loose the chains of injustice" (Isa 58:6). "You trample on the heads of the poor . . . and deny justice to the oppressed," cried Amos (2:7). "The more the priests increased, the more they sinned against me," wrote Hosea (4:7). "They covet fields and seize them, and houses, and take them . . . and defraud a fellowman of his inheritance" (Micah 2:2).

Isaiah 61:1-4 says,

> "The Spirit of the Sovereign LORD is on me,
>   because the Lord has anointed me
>   to proclaim good news to the poor.
> He has sent me to bind up the brokenhearted,
>   to proclaim freedom for the captives
>   and release from darkness for the prisoners,
> to proclaim the year of the LORD's favor."

Isaiah 61 is known as the prominent passage that identifies the coming Messiah as one who would bring "good news to the poor."

"I will not turn back my wrath," was the repeated reminder of God. Because of his very nature, there was no way he could turn a blind eye to injustice. Ethics were the expression of faith, not an optional choice. How the Israelites related to their own people was built into the covenant that God made with them. And the longer the injustices lasted and the deeper they took root, the sooner judgment would come. The result of Israel and Judah's disregarding of the poor was captivity by Assyria and eventually Babylon.

Hardness of heart that leads to moral, ethical, and religious failure cannot be casually ignored. Thousands of years later, God's people continue to fall prey to their proclivity for desiring wealth and power at the expense of the poor and oppressed. Christians and Christian churches, like those in the eighth century B.C., still get lulled into cultural complicity and remain silent in the face of injustice. God has not changed, and he still hears the cries of injustice. Where are the prophets who are God's spokespersons on behalf of the weak, the estranged, the hungry, and the ignored in our own culture of affluence?

Isaiah prophesized that God's wrath would come on their nation, that he would remove his light because of the religious Israelite's false humility as they failed to share their food and clothing, offer shelter to the homeless, pay wages to their laborers, and ignore the needs of their own countrymen. Other prophets, including Jeremiah, Micah, and Hosea, condemned the duplicity of the rich and religious. Amos, in particular, confronted the injustices of businessmen in the market square for "trampling on the heads of the poor" through ill-conceived sales methods, paying off judges for favor, and unethical behavior against their kinsmen (Amos 2:7).

The Second Testament

The Gospels

The four Gospels undeniably confront even a casual reader with this symbiotic relationship of wealth and eternity. The stories of Lazarus, of the condemned rich man who ignored the hungry beggar under his table, of the rich man who built bigger barns and gave favoritism to the rich, of the unpredictable salvation of the tax collector, Zacchaeus, and the condemnation of the "goats" by Jesus to those who did not "see" and respond to the hungry, the thirsty, the naked, the stranger, the sick, and the imprisoned. All of these will be explored more in depth in later chapters.

Each of the Gospel writers focused on the critical theme of bringing God's kingdom to earth. Interpersonal relationships were to be based on the teaching and actions of Jesus, loving God and one's neighbor intimately at the same time. Matthew focused on discipleship in the reign of God, framed by the Sermon on the Mount. Following Jesus meant bearing fruit and resisting hypocrisy with a stern warning that "not everyone who says to me, 'Lord, Lord,' shall enter the kingdom of heaven, but only he who does the will of my Father" (Matt 7:21). His will included baptizing and teaching others to be disciples.

Mark's Gospel tells the story of the widow's offering. "Jesus sat down opposite the place where the offerings were put and watched the crowd putting their money into the temple treasury. Many rich people threw in large amounts. But a poor widow came and put in two very small copper coins, worth only a fraction of a penny. Calling his disciples to him, Jesus said, 'I tell you the truth, this poor widow has put more into the treasury than all the others. They gave out of their wealth; but she, out of her poverty, put in everything—all she had to live on" (Mark 12:41-44).

The Gospel of Luke and the book of Acts are particularly concerned with issues of wealth, poverty, and relationships in the kingdom of God. Jesus' confirmation of his Messiahship was based on his reading of Isaiah's prophecy stating that concern for the poor and marginalized was foundational to recognizing the long-awaited Lord. Luke records the account of Jesus returning to the synagogue in his hometown of Nazareth and being asked to read Isaiah 61:1-2 from the scroll. "The Spirit of the Sovereign Lord is upon me, because he has anointed me to preach good news to the poor. He has sent me to bind up the brokenhearted, to proclaim freedom to the captives, and release from darkness to the prisoners, to proclaim the year of the Lord's favor." Luke then says all the eyes turned to look at Jesus as he sat down. "Today, this scripture is fulfilled in your hearing" (Luke 4:21). Luke clearly affirms that Jesus is fulfilling the promise of the long-awaited Savior, recognized by his role in caring for the poor and disenfranchised. Bringing good news to the poor is a significant Messianic motif in both Luke and Acts. From the very beginning of Mary's awareness of the coming holy birth of the awaited Messiah, her hymn of praise, the Magnificat in Luke 1:46-55, affirms God's favor for the poor and hatred for the rich who oppress them. Her words of the coming kingdom challenge the rich and powerful, who "are sent away empty handed" (Luke 1:53). Years later John the Baptist breaks onto the scene as a wilderness prophet of low socioeconomic status, calling for actions that are keeping with repentance. "What should we do, then?" the crowd asked. John answered, "The man with two coats should share one who has none, and the one who has food should do the same" (Luke 3:11).

Luke also shares Jesus' parable about the rich fool whose plan to tear down his smaller barns after a record grain harvest to build bigger barns and "take life easy, eat drink and be merry" ends abruptly in his unexpected death (Luke 12:19). "This is how it will be with anyone who stores up things for himself, but is not rich toward God" (Luke 12:21). "He is addressed as a fool, not because he has possessions, but because he is devoid of piety toward God, consideration for his neighbor and regard for his true well-being" (Gillman 1991, 76).

Giving invitation to the uninvited is yet another profound kingdom lesson shared by Luke. Jesus tells two parables of hypocrisy and excuses given at tables of the rich and famous. In the first parable, the host reminds his guests they will be humiliated if they scramble for the distinguished seats at the table, thus encouraging them to "take the lowest place," allowing the host to move them up to a place of honor, "for everyone who exalts himself will be humbled, and he who humbles himself will be exalted" (Luke 14:11). In the second parable, Jesus notes the traditions of the rich to invite each other to festive gatherings and ignore the "little people" who were disenfranchised from the wealthy. Yet when each potential guest had excuses for why they could not attend, "the owner of the house became angry and ordered his servant, 'Go out quickly into the streets and alleys of the town and bring the poor, the crippled, the blind and the lame'" (Luke 14:21). In an ironic reversal, the rich are now excluded from the Great Banquet.

John declares, "If anyone has material possessions and sees a brother or sister in need but has no pity on them, how can the love of God be in that person?" (1 John 3:17).

Acts and the Early Church

As Luke shares the history of the early church in Acts, there are numerous examples of how the Spirit-filled church uses their possessions. The descending of the Spirit at Pentecost led to the physical manifestation of a new social order "devoted to the apostles' teaching and fellowship, breaking bread and praying, sharing everything in common, selling their possessions and goods to give to anyone who had need" (Acts 2:42-47). Because the "believers were one in heart and mind," there were no needy persons among them (Acts 4:32-34). The early church was a giving church, frequently noted for its generosity to poorer churches facing famine and struggle, "each according to their ability" (Acts 11:29). They took care of the poor and widows (Acts 6). Sacrificial giving was a core expectation. Barnabas even sold a field he owned and placed it at the apostles' feet (Acts 4:36-37). While the Apostle Peter made it clear no one had to sell their possessions, deceit and false piety were forbidden, so much so that when Ananias and Sapphira sold their land and quietly held back some of the proceeds, they were struck down and died (Acts 5:5). "Great fear seized the whole church and all who heard about these events" (Acts 5:11). Luke clearly shows that, like with Judas, "Satan can get control of one's decision-making capacity" (Gillman 1991, 98). Even as Simon the Magician offered money to the apostles to get their miraculous skills (Acts 8:9-24), and the owners of a slave girl used her divination for profit making (Acts 16:16-24), all are rebuked for trying to obtain these talents for selfish gain. Readers see how quickly the wealthy seek to gain God's favor without having to know God.

Paul's Letters

The Apostle Paul began his missionary tours after the Jerusalem Church sent him out to the Gentiles with one mandate: "All they asked was that we should continue to remember the poor, the very thing I had been eager to do all along" (Gal 2:10). He frequently collected offerings from more wealthy churches to help those who struggled. Paul not only kept his word to remember the poor, but he personally became poor during many points throughout his ministry, experiencing hunger, lack of clothing, sickness, loneliness, and even imprisonment. "To this very hour we go hungry and thirsty, we are in rags, we are brutally treated, we are homeless" (1 Cor 4:11). In the midst of such difficult circumstances, Paul recognized that Jesus had chosen to become poor for our sake. "For you know the grace of our Lord Jesus Christ, that though he was rich, yet for your sake he became poor, so that you through his poverty might become rich" (2 Cor 8:9). Contentment comes with the basics of life and has nothing to do with the world and riches. "For we brought nothing into the world, and we can take nothing out of it. But if we have food and clothing, we will be content with that. People who want to get rich fall into temptation and a trap and into many foolish and harmful desires that plunge men into ruin and destruction. For the love of money is a root of all kinds of evil. Some people, eager for money, have wandered from the faith and pierced themselves with many griefs" (1 Tim 6:6-10). "Furthermore, just as they did not think it worthwhile to retain the knowledge of God, so God gave them over to a depraved mind, so that they do what ought not to be done" (Rom 1:28).

General Letters: Hebrews, James, Peter, and John's letters

The book of James boldly confronts the hypocrites, saying, "Suppose there are brothers or sisters who need clothes and don't have enough to eat. What good is there in your saying to them, 'God bless you! Keep warm and eat well!' if you don't give them the necessities of life? In the same way, faith by itself, if it is not accompanied by action, is dead" (Jas 2:15-17).

The Revelation of John

In the book of Revelation, the Apocalypse of John, the churches were judged in the same way as our contemporary churches. The wealthy church in Laodicea saw itself as rich and without need, but was destined to be "spewed out of God's mouth" for being lukewarm in God's eyes, unable to recognize they were actually "wretched, pitiful, poor, blind and naked" (Rev 3:17). A lukewarm church that is neither hot nor cold is unacceptable in the kingdom of God. The church in Ephesus had its lampstand removed by the angel because it had lost its first love. Yet the Church in Smyrna, financially poor and afflicted (Rev 2:9), was called "rich" by God and promised the crown of life as they remained faithful.

6
THE BIBLE AND HISTORY

A Brief Sweep of Major Movements

Pre-Christian Foundations

Prior to the advent of Christ, Aristotle (384–322 B.C.) concluded that happiness was the ultimate purpose of life. However, the way to achieve happiness was through virtuous living obtained by conscious exertion or activity toward purposeful being. His being-in-action approach requires wisdom, the highest human virtue, which leads to reflection and discernment. To be happy, seeking wealth comes through the management of one's household so the family can enjoy a good life. Accumulating wealth for wealth itself does not lead to happiness. Instead, becoming generous givers to one's friends is virtuous, unlike those who are "vulgar," spending money on that which is not beautiful, with a desire for bringing attention to themselves.

Early Christian Views

After the resurrection of Christ, the early Christians were mostly directed by their Jewish background and the teachings of Jesus, the Apostles, and writers of the Epistles. While the Roman Empire swallowed the world with its wealth and power,

Christians deepened their resolve to live as "resident aliens," in the world but not of it. The church was loving, even to pagans, hospitable to strangers, and generous to the poor. "Despite persecution and disadvantages in their social situation, the Christian population was growing because the early Church attracted people in the early Roman Empire. The greatest attractions were Christians' practices and behaviors. An essential part of Christian communities depended on their willingness to aid those in need and on the teachings of the Christian church about the right use of material goods" (Inoue 2017, 7). In the midst of the oppressive Roman government, driven by their wealth and power, "Christians revitalized life in Greco-Roman cities by providing new norms and new kinds of social relationships able to cope with many urgent urban problems. To cities filled with the homeless, impoverished, and strangers, Christians offered an immediate basis for attachments. To cities filled with orphans and widows, Christians provided a new and expanded sense of family. To cities torn by violent ethnic strife, Christians offered a new basis for social solidarity. And to cities faced with epidemic, fires and earthquakes, Christians offered effective nursing services" (Stark 1996, 161).

Church Fathers

In the patristic age to follow, theology and interpretation of the Bible continued. Church Fathers, such as Augustine of Hippo (354–430 A.D.), had significant theological and philosophical impact on Western Christianity. Augustine sold his patrimony and gave the money to the poor, saying followers of Christ should not seek wealth as a worthy goal. In his sermon to the rich he said, "That bread which you keep, belongs to the hungry; that coat which you preserve in your wardrobe, to the naked; those shoes which are rotting in your possession, to the shoeless; that gold which you have hidden in the ground, to the needy. Wherefore, as often as you were able to help others, and refused, so often did you do them wrong."

Other Church Fathers were likewise direct in their views of the impact of the rich on the poor. In 300 A.D., Cyprian penned these words: "The property of the wealthy holds them in chains . . . which shackle their courage and choke their faith and hamper their judgment and throttle their souls. They think of themselves as owners, whereas it is they rather who are owned: enslaved as they are to their own property, they are not the masters of their money but its slaves."

Basil of Caesarea (330–370 A.D.) wrote, "How can I make you realize the misery of the poor? How can I make you understand that your wealth comes from their weeping?" John Chrysostom (347–407 A.D.) wrote, "The rich are in possession of the goods of the poor, even if they have acquired them honestly or inherited them legally."

The Middle Ages: "Dark Ages"

The medieval period (fifth century through the fifteenth century) of European history, between the fall of the Roman Empire and the beginning of the Renaissance, is sometimes referred to as the "Dark Ages." Over 200 million people died from the Black Death amid a feudal system that left little hope for the poor. During the early Middle Ages poverty was normative and only a few had financial wealth. Those that possessed financial wealth were also considered more holy. Helping the poor was a sign of holiness as well. By the High Middle Ages of the twelfth century, ironically, an upturn in wealth began to occur. Even peasants began to break out of the stranglehold of poverty. For followers of Christ, no longer was wealth associated with holiness. Now poverty itself became a sign of holiness and generosity, particularly emphasized by the new monastic orders, including the Franciscans, who refused to live like the wealthier bishops and growing aristocracy.

In the Late Middle Ages, the poet-philosopher Dante Alighieri wrote his classical work *Inferno*, considered the finest poem of the era. The impressive work was a collaboration of classical and medieval beliefs called *The Divine Comedy*, an allegory about a nine-layered journey through purgatory, heaven, and hell of the soul of man toward God. The purpose, Dante wrote, was to convert a corrupt society to righteousness, and "to remove those living in this life from a state of misery and lead them to a state of felicity." In particular, the sin of wantonness, "unduly lavish and without restraint," was the most reprehensible. It was like Aristotle's idea of knowing virtue but not having the internal controls to overcome vice and practice these virtues. Dante saw it as the sin that led to deeper levels of hell. For Augustine, wantonness was not so much a problem of knowledge but of the will to overcome it, as humans tend to choose lesser values over greater goods regularly. Dante takes the idea even further, suggesting the lack of advocacy to help others in God's realm condemns mankind to "the hottest places in hell reserved for those who, in times of great moral crisis, maintain their neutrality."

Wantonness, though not a common word today, accurately describes much of the American culture. The etymology of the fourteenth-century word means "deficient of discipline." Self-indulgent, pampered, spoiled, hard-hearted, affluent, unfeeling, or lacking compassion are the synonyms of the undisciplined that lead to various levels of hell.

Monasticism

Early monasticism was an ongoing expression of faithfulness to God through simplicity and solitude. Though not mentioned in the Bible, becoming a monk was not only a visible sign of denouncing worldly goods, but a spiritual vocation completely devoted to God. St. Anthony (252–356 A.D.), one of the earliest known monks, roamed the Egyptian desert as a hermit and is credited as the patron saint of the Orthodox Church. Raised by rich and noble parents, he found himself compelled to obey Christ's command in Matthew's Gospel: "If you wish to be perfect, go, sell your possessions, and give the money to the poor, and you will have treasure in heaven; then come, follow me" (Matt 19:21).

St. Francis of Assisi (1181–1226), an iconic monk in the late Middle Ages, challenged older orders of monks to live in extreme simplicity and volunteer poverty. This patron saint of animals and ecology has impacted countless followers of God through his lifestyle of simplicity and chosen poverty. Voluntary poverty was greatly admired in the High Middle Ages, and Francis urged his followers to live by wandering and begging, not even keeping an apple overnight to eat the next day, unless hungry. Otherwise it was to be given away. As profound an example the Franciscan order has had on latter Christians, they were unable to maintain the same extremism after his death, living mostly like austere monks.

Ignatius of Loyola (1491–1564), like Aquinas, was born into nobility and also chose to abandon his worldly privilege to take a vow of physical poverty. Through deep spiritual exercises that directed him and his companions in the Society of Jesus (Jesuits), life was focused on loving God shared with meaningful companionship. That lifestyle of spiritual poverty was to look like that of Jesus, simple and caring for people instead of things. Ignatius encouraged those seeking God's will to have a spiritual director to help them discern the questions of life.

Thomas Aquinas (1225–1274) grew up with wealth, possessions, and power but chose to abandon them. While he agreed with Aristotle that happiness was the ultimate goal of life, his deep Christian faith expected happiness in the next life. It is through charity, the highest virtue, that we discover how to love others in God. Donors should give liberally from their surplus, that which is needed to sustain life, and whatever possible to extreme needs. Such a lifestyle brings the most "fruits" and joy. He recognized that money brings more power and begins to look like happiness, though it never leads to infinite happiness. Wanting more than is needed becomes covetousness, which upsets the real order of love and leads to vices.

The Crusades

Between 1096 and 1291, as many as eight major Crusades took place. The bloody, violent, and often ruthless conflicts propelled the status of European Christians.

The Christian Crusades against Muslims in the eleventh to thirteenth centuries were church-sanctioned quests that have had a chilling impact on the actions of Christians against others who do not share their views. In 1095, Pope Urban II preached a sermon assuring the soldiers it was God's will to take away Muslim control of Jerusalem as part of a religious pilgrimage experience, not only to gain forgiveness of sins for the Crusaders, but to give permission to take from their conquered enemies any possessions or land they owned since God was on their side. Thus, giving to others in need did not include the enemies that Jesus had called Christians to love. In fact, it was even "Christian" to take from them. The Muslims deserved their fate. Unfortunately, some of the roots and language of modern missions were born out of the Crusades when conquering the enemy at all costs was blessed with divine sanction.

The Renaissance

At the end of the fourteenth century, the Italian leaders of their city-states announced the end of the Middle Ages and the rebirth of society, named the Gilded Age. For close to three centuries science, inventions, poetry, art, architecture, and societal norms were open for change. Humanism emerged, putting mankind at the center of the universe and encouraging people to be curious and questioning, even questioning the established church that had become mired in corruption and scandal. The middle class grew, luxurious homes were built, and clothes identified one's status. Many poor people lived on farms, wore simple clothes, and ate basic food such as bread or soup made from scraps. Their homes were usually very small, sometimes only having one room. No longer seen through Christian eyes, the poor during the Renaissance were identified by socio-economic classes. The "helpless poor" were the invalids, mentally ill, and aged who received government help. The next class, about a fifth of the population, was known as the "have-nothings" (*miserabili*), including people such as laborers, porters, journeymen, and out-of-work servants. In normal times they could scrape by, but they had no savings. Sudden increases in the price of bread or downturns in the economy could make them dependent upon charity. A third class of the poor included craft workers, shop-keepers, and minor officials, usually respected in society. Forms of class identification came to diminish and replace the views of the church and early Christians.

The Poor Laws

By the early 1500s, many towns and some nations tried to coordinate their systems of relief for the poor. They made efforts to restrict begging, conduct a census of the local poor, and provide training and work for the unemployed. The Poor Law system was codified as early as 1536 and was in existence for several centuries, until the emergence of the modern welfare state after World War II. The laws were designed to contribute to the general good of the people in need, as well as maintain order amongst growing social issues. Those considered vagrants, the involuntarily unemployed, the helpless, and the neediest, such as the aged, disabled, and very sick, could receive financial help, but those who could work were required by local authorities to find work. They had to become apprentices and return to their local parishes or risk being punished through fines or workhouse confinement. Tools and materials were made available for the poor workers. The laws allowed the government to raise taxes for the initiative if needed. In 1834 the New Poor Laws changed supervision to a central system. Moreover, attitudes of the general public changed remarkably from the early days. While at one point the poor were essentially considered victims of their situation and their relief a Christian duty, the growing view became that they were largely responsible for their own situation and they could change it if they chose to do so.

The Reformations: Protestant (1517–1648), Catholic, and Radical

In 1517 Martin Luther posted his "95 Theses" on the Wittenberg church door. What had been brewing for years now became a movement. The Protestant Reformation was the sixteenth-century religious movement that caused the political and cultural upheaval that splintered the long-established Catholic dynasty in Europe. Reformers sought to purify the church and reestablish a belief that the Bible, not tradition, should be the sole source of spiritual authority. They argued for a religious and political redistribution of power into the hands of Bible pastors and princes. The disruption triggered wars, persecutions, and a Counter-Reformation by the Catholic Church.

Alongside these things, it brought significant changes in how the church viewed wealth and giving. Luther and Calvin restored a high value of work, challenging the escapist lifestyles of the monks, to include God's vocational call to daily employment in whatever "station" they were in.

Anabaptists determined that neither the Protestant Reformation nor the Catholics' changes were enough. Convinced that the New Testament church should be separated from any support and connection to the Catholic Church, they continued to seek additional church reforms based on a more communal lifestyle with deep ethical behavior, simplicity, and accountability. As a countercultural example of nonviolence, love, and care, Anabaptists, including Mennonites, Swiss Brethren, Amish, and German Baptists, sought to attract the poor and others seeking a better lifestyle as a "light on the hillside" and example of Christian compassion. This emphasis on the church as a sign of the kingdom helps explain the Anabaptist insistence on mutual aid and hearing each other's burdens to care for each other's emotional, social, spiritual, material, and physical needs.

The Great Awakening (1730s–1740s)

A series of Great Awakenings impacted the English colonies and England following the Enlightenment's "Age of Reason," which had diminished zeal in Christian faith in favor of secular thinking and nationalism. Christian leaders like Jonathan Edwards, John Wesley, and George Whitefield often traveled from town to town, preaching the Gospel, emphasizing salvation from sins, and promoting enthusiasm for Christianity. John Wesley practiced what he preached, as he promoted the social implications of Christian faith. He fought against the slave trade, worked to deal with unemployment, advocated for prison reform, and created loans for the poor and medicine for the sick. He even gave away considerable amounts of his own money to people in need.

"The Great Reversal" (1900–1930)

Christian history is filled with moving examples of Christians not only serving the poor and marginalized, but also addressing some of the root causes of the social issues which oppressed them. The integration of bringing good news through salvation also included good news of social action which proclaimed God's kingdom. "The Great Reversal," a term coined by historian Timothy L. Smith, refers to the switchback evangelicals made in the early part of this century from evangelical social concern to individualism. "The early church, both in England and America, was noted for its social involvement, establishing welfare societies such as the Salvation Army, schools for immigrants, homes for unwed mothers, city missions, and agencies to help the poor, the sick, prisoners, and other needy folk. The church supported legislation to bring about social justice" (Moberg 1972, 185–86).

As American individualism and personal goals of success and prosperity grew among Christians, and as a more liberal "Social Gospel" theology, championed by Walter Rauschenbusch, gained traction amongst liberals, conservative Christians disassociated themselves. For conservatives it became increasingly difficult for them to see the evils encroaching on society. Personal piety was the focus. The problem is that personal piety rarely positively impacts society.

What became known as The Great Reversal (1900–1930) separated the church for thirty years. But in time, efforts to bring these extreme platforms to a more centrist acceptance that acknowledged God embraced some of each view. At the First Lausanne Congress, a global gathering in 1974 of evangelical

Christian leaders from 150 nations, they gave their concluding statement about Christians and Social Responsibility:

"Although reconciliation with other people is not reconciliation with God, nor is social action evangelism, nor is political liberation salvation, nevertheless we affirm that evangelism and socio-political involvement are both part of our Christian duty. For both are necessary expressions of our doctrines of God and Man, our love for our neighbour and our obedience to Jesus Christ. The message of salvation implies also a message of judgment upon every form of alienation, oppression and discrimination, and we should not be afraid to denounce evil and injustice wherever they exist. When people receive Christ, they are born again into his kingdom and must seek not only to exhibit but also to spread its righteousness in the midst of an unrighteous world. The salvation we claim should be transforming us in the totality of our personal and social responsibilities. Faith without works is dead" (The Lausanne Movement 1974).

Biblical Views of Wealth and Poverty Supported

In more modern times, the European colonialism that often went to conquer new lands coopted the church and teaching of Jesus as a defense of their "God-given" right and call. In time economic and social systems like capitalism, the Industrial Revolution, Marxism, socialism, and secularism were intertwined with religious and nonreligious viewpoints to ameliorate the cultural norms. As one would expect, Christianity was synthesized by these emerging cultures.

In recent decades, the United States came to prominence as one of the wealthiest nations in the history of mankind. Economists would mostly agree some of those reasons are earned and some just given. Regardless, the sustained higher rate of real GDP growth has resulted in a substantially higher level of wealth per person in the United States than in other major industrial countries. With a historical Judeo-Christian underpinning, God easily gets praised as the reason for such economic blessings. For many, God has blessed America because we bless him. Some churches raise the United States flag along with the Christian flag on their sanctuary stages as a statement that our economic standard and blessings are from God. In other churches the so-called "Prosperity Gospel" takes things to the next level, teaching that if the poor or sick would just obey the Bible, the evidence of their faith would be economic gain and physical blessings since God wants everyone to be rich and whole. Christian nationalism amplifies these ideas and melds itself to theological conservatism, more often evangelicalism. In all of these, the belief that "God is on our side" dominates. Those who are not Christian, wealthy, and salute the American flag cannot be blessed, or at least not as much as those who do.

Five Christian Approaches

Though it is challenging to categorize and reduce disparate views through the ages, perhaps five of them offer clear differences from which Christians can categorize contrasting views.

Wealth Is No Longer an Issue in Christian Faith Because of Grace

The Apostle Paul proclaimed, "For it is by grace you have been saved, through faith—and this is not from yourselves, it is the gift of God, not by works, so that no one can boast" (Eph 2:8-9). "Sola fide" (faith alone) is clearly taught in the Bible. No amount of charity can get one into heaven. Yet others, like James, would argue that "faith without works is dead" (2:17-18). Both Paul and James seem to agree in other passages that true faith exemplifies itself in good works. The question John asks is, "If anyone has material possessions and sees a brother or sister in need but has no pity on them, how can the love of God be in that person?" (1 John 3:17). Jesus said that the Great Commandment integrates loving God and loving one's neighbor, making his point with the parable of the Good Samaritan. While each of these verses are correct, one's interpretation of them may miss the essence of the good news of salvation. Obviously Jesus' strong words to the rich young ruler to go and sell everything and come follow him must be considered. Is that what it takes to become a Christian?

Wealth Ownership Ignores and Offends Christian Faith

There is a branch of Christianity that views the wealthy man as extremely sinful, standing on the wrong side of the gospel. According to historian Alan S. Kahan, the day of judgment is viewed as a time when "the social order will be turned upside down and . . . the poor will turn out to be the ones truly blessed" (Kahan 2009, 43). Thomas Aquinas taught that "greed is a sin against God, just as all mortal sins, in as much as man condemns things eternal for the sake of temporal things." The Manicheans of the third century believed the physical world was innately evil and participation in its pleasures meant condemnation. Only the spiritual world, entered by renouncing material and worldly goods and pleasures as Jesus commanded his disciples, would bring eternal peace. The ascetic life of voluntary poverty was an outward sign by serious Christians of the known evil of wealth and power.

Wealth Ownership Stifles Christian Faith

Jesus proclaimed hard words to the wealthy and to his own disciples. "How hard it is for the rich to enter the kingdom of God!" With a powerful metaphor he said, "Children, how hard it is to enter the kingdom of God! It is easier for a camel to go through the eye of a needle than for someone who is rich to enter the kingdom of God" (Mark 10:23-25).

Like several well-known theologians, Martin Luther taught that "mammon" was the primary idol of culture, noting Jesus' encounter with the rich young ruler to give up his wealth as an obstacle to faith. New Testament passages regarding the dangers of wealth are frequent: "people who want to get rich fall into temptation and a trap and into many foolish and harmful desires that plunge men into ruin and destruction," that "the love of money is the root of all evil" (1 Tim 6:1).

Some Bible scholars note that it is the love of money that is the obstacle to faith, not the money itself. Yet amassing material wealth on earth instead of heaven was discouraged for true disciples. "Do not store up for yourselves treasures on earth, where moth and rust destroy, and where thieves break in and steal. But store up for yourselves treasures in heaven, where moth and rust do not destroy, and where thieves do not break in and steal. For where your treasure is, there your heart will be also" (Matt 6:19-21).

Jesus urges his followers to remove from their lives those things which cause them to sin, saying, "If your hand causes you to sin, cut it off. It is better for you to enter life maimed than to go with two hands into hell, where the fire never goes out" (Mark 9:43). In order to remove the desire for wealth and material possessions as an obstacle to faith, some Christians have taken voluntary vows of poverty and various forms of asceticism, charity, and almsgiving. Even personal ownership of common items like cars, housing, businesses, and saving accounts have been considered idolatrous, especially when such items can be shared with others.

In this view moderation in all things becomes the normative principle for Christians.

Wealth Ownership Is Primarily for Generosity

A completely different view of wealth emphasized that pursuing it for the right reason was not only acceptable, but commendable. Puritans, Calvinists, and some Protestants celebrated hard work and moderate lifestyles as their Christian duty. These approaches viewed the pursuit of wealth not only as acceptable, but as a religious spiritual calling or duty. Englishman and revivalist John Wesley was a strong proponent of gaining wealth to "gain all you can, save all you can and give all you can." Because it is impossible to give charitably if one is poor, John Wesley and his Methodists were noted for their consistently large contributions to charity in the form of churches, hospitals, and schools.

Wealth Prosperity Is a Sign of God's Blessing

A relatively new approach to defending wealth accumulation emerged from contemporary preachers and authors who propound prosperity theology, teaching that God promises wealth and abundance to those who will believe in him and follow his laws. Sometimes called the "health and wealth gospel," advocates of the prosperity gospel say that the Bible teaches that financial blessing is the will of God for Christians. While often tied to televangelists and positive-only preachers, generous donations to their philanthropies are a sign or way of increasing personal blessing.

Prosperity theology first came to prominence during the "Healing Revivals" in the 1950s. In the 1990s and 2000s, it became accepted by many influential leaders in the charismatic movement and has been promoted by Christian missionaries throughout the world. However, much of the movement has been harshly criticized by leaders of mainstream Christians as a nonscriptural doctrine and outright heresy.

However, a softer version of this ideology has also emerged among mainstream Christian thinking. It is often tied to provincialism and nationalism, suggesting that God has blessed America because he finds special favor for the United States as a "chosen nation," similar to Old Testament Israel. With the Christian flag hung alongside the American flag on church platforms, the belief is that his favor blesses the Christian wealthy and powerful because of the nation's Judeo-Christian views, numerous churches, national prosperity, and superiority compared to other nations.

Your View?

Because one's presuppositions shape one's personal worldview, it is important to reflect on these views. Acknowledging that Christians do not necessarily think "Christianly," it is sometimes hard for "cultural Christians" to dig deeper into their own beliefs. Many "successful" Christians have never focused on what they believe. Others have mixed them together in some kind of theological salad and not realized how one view negates the other. To believe that wealth is an offense to faith, yet spend the majority of one's life and energy around wealth accumulation is hypocrisy. To believe that seeking wealth is for the sake of generosity to others yet only give token amounts to charities and the poor is hypocrisy as well. Recognizing that biblical "moderation" is a basic principle for Christ-followers, yet owning big houses, boats, cars, expensive clothing, and taking exotic vacations, is inconsistent with that principle. Believing that one's wealth results as a type of American birthright does not answer the question of why our nation has so many citizens living in poverty since they, too, are Americans.

Clearly one's foundational views of wealth and poverty drive each person, whether they acknowledge it or not. That view is often based on what one does and then justifies, not what they say they believe. Personal inconsistencies between one's beliefs and actions are one thing, but personal deceit that perpetuates lies is the greater evil. The work of the Holy Spirit is to confront the hypocrisy, offer healing, and provide direction. One of the biggest needs for wealthy Christians is to detox from their lifestyle long enough to spend quality time studying and examining their core beliefs and actions based on a biblical worldview and the teachings of Jesus. Years of avoidance, justification, and apathy often define our lives and ultimately harden our hearts.

7

WHO THEN CAN BE SAVED?

Profound Warnings That May "Scare the Hell Out of You"

Read in isolated passages throughout the Bible, a seeker of God's will may only feel a twinge of alarm at the somewhat blunt verses that challenge a follower to recognize the danger of riches. However, when read as a simple list, the biblical warnings about the dangers of wealth are overwhelming:

Woe to the rich. "Woe to you who are rich, for you have already received your comfort. Woe to you who are well fed now, for you will go hungry. Woe to you who laugh now, for you will mourn and weep. Woe to you when everyone speaks well of you, for that is how their ancestors treated the false prophets" (Luke 6:24-26).

Who then can be saved? "'Again I tell you, it is easier for a camel to go through the eye of a needle than for someone who is rich to enter the kingdom of God.' When the disciples heard this, they were greatly astonished and asked, 'Who then can be saved?'" (Matt 19:24-25).

Eternal punishment? "'I tell you the truth, whatever you did not do for the least of these, you did not do for me.' Then they will go away to eternal punishment, but the righteous to eternal life" (Matt 25:45-46).

Cannot serve two masters. "You cannot serve both God and money" (Matt 6:24).

Itching ears? "For the time will come when people will not put up with sound doctrine. Instead, to suit their own desires, they will gather around them a great number of teachers to say what their itching ears want to hear" (2 Tim 4:3).

Fattened yourselves for the day of slaughter. "Now listen, you rich people, weep and wail because of the misery that is coming upon you. Your wealth has rotted, and moths have eaten your clothes. Your gold and silver are corroded. Their corrosion will testify against you and eat your flesh like fire. You have hoarded wealth in the last days. Look, the wages you failed to pay the workmen who mowed your fields are crying out against you. The cries of the harvesters have reached the ears of the Lord Almighty. You have lived on earth in luxury and self-indulgence. You have fattened yourselves in the day of slaughter" (Jas 5:1-5).

Wandered from the faith. "For the love of money is a root of all kinds of evil. Some people, eager for money have wandered from the faith and pierced themselves with many griefs" (1 Tim 3:10).

Life is more important than your body. "Do not worry about your life, what you will eat or drink, or about your body, what you will wear. Is not life more important than food and the body more important than clothes?" (Matt 6:25).

Bigger barns, easy life, yet you will get what you deserve. "I will say to myself, 'I have plenty of good things laid up for many years. Take life easy; eat, drink and be merry.' But God will say to you, 'You fool! This very night your very life will be demanded from you'" (Luke 12:19-20).

Insulting God. "Those who oppress the poor insult their Maker, but helping the poor honors him" (Prov 14:31).

Self-deception. "The rich man is wise in his own eyes, but the poor who has understanding sees through him" (Prov 28:11).

Unconcerned. "Now this was the sin of your sister Sodom: She and her daughters were arrogant, overfed and unconcerned; they did not help the poor and needy. They were haughty and did detestable things before me. Therefore, I did away with them as you have seen" (Ezek 16:49-50).

It's more than saying "Lord." "Not everyone who calls me 'Lord, Lord' will enter the kingdom of heaven" (Matt 7:21).

Sent to Hell for Not Seeing or Caring?

Many Americans have never had the opportunity to travel into nations with significant poverty, often feeling little obligation to care for the world's poor who they have not personally seen. Many have never seen any of the 726 million people living in extreme poverty, surviving on less than $1.90 a day or the 3 billion people existing on less than $2.50 a day. In fact, for many Americans "out of sight, out of mind" is the way we live. Many would even say that we have enough of our own poor and needy, and don't have to fix the world's problems. Yet the huge and wealthy majority do little, if anything, for the poor and marginalized within their own nation.

In the United States:

- 39.7 million are poor, about 12 percent of the total population. Over 40 million experience food insecurity.
- 2.2 million adults are incarcerated, more than in any other nation.
- 50 thousand people were sex trafficked last year.
- An estimated 10 million Americans annually experience domestic violence.
- Almost one half of our nation live with a chronic disease.
- Over half a million go homeless each night in the U.S.
- 3 million legal refugees have been resettled here since 1975.

Have You Seen Them? What Are Their Names?

While Jesus frequently spoke to the masses, several of his most profound teachings were directed to his disciples. Five of his deep discussions with them were held at the Mount of Olives. Just a few days before the Passover, Jesus was teaching the Twelve about the coming kingdom in heaven and the glory of the Son of Man, as well as about the final judgment (Matt 25:31-46).

Jesus said, "As a shepherd separates the sheep from the goats, so he will put the sheep on his right, to receive his blessed inheritance and kingdom prepared for them since the beginning of creation. But to the goats on his left he will say, 'Depart from me, you who are cursed, into the eternal fire prepared for the devil and his angels'" (Matt 25:41).

Why? While the New Testament is built around the principles of God's unmerited favor, there are only a few passages that seem to focus on works. This is one of them. Jesus' words are a clear admonishment to his disciples that good news to the least of these included actions of mercy. The goats did nothing to help them because they did not see the hungry, the thirsty, the stranger, the naked, the sick, and the imprisoned. The evidence of their spiritual blindness manifested itself by inaction and apathy. Yet seeing the needs of the least without compassionate acts of assistance is also spiritual death in God. Seeing and doing are holistically integrated in the life of a follower of Jesus. "Do not merely listen to the word, and so deceive yourselves. Do what it says" (Jas 1:22). James goes on to say, "Religion that God our Father accepts as pure and faultless is this: to look after orphans and widows in their distress and to keep oneself from being polluted by the world" (1:27). There is no "half-gospel" that divides believing and doing, especially toward the most vulnerable ones.

Spiritual blindness has eternal significance. Not seeing the speed limit does not mean we are not accountable to follow it. The very nature of how God created us included an intuitive knowledge that others matter. Yet self-centered lifestyles distort God's image in us to not even see what he sees, much less care for that which he cares. Yet it seems that the extreme punishment does not match the "crime." In immediate defense, we turn to verses like, "For it is by grace you have been saved, through faith, and this is not from yourselves; it is the gift of God, not by works, so that no one can boast" (Eph 2:8-9). How could both be true?

God cares deeply for those in need. Not seeing and not caring is not an option for a follower of Jesus with a biblical worldview. God cares that the hungry are fed, the thirsty are given drink, the stranger gets invited in, the sick are cared for, and the imprisoned are visited. He cares for the poor, the marginalized, the widow, and the orphan. Regardless of one's theology, the poor and marginalized significantly matter to God. To be Christian is to integrate faith and works and not be polluted by the world's values. Judgement follows for those who do not do this.

Two heresies often emerge here. Because our relationship is not transactional, doing good deeds to receive salvation is not an option. We can never be good enough to overcome the sin that separates humankind from a holy God. At the same time, "getting God" is not a free ticket into heaven, after which I can then do what I want for the rest of my life. Unmerited favor is not about cheap grace. Saying "yes" to Christ as Lord should radicalize my desire to serve and follow him. Following him is costly and hard, but brings fulfillment and joy like no worldly pleasure can. The reality is that salvation through God's grace, at some level, is a dynamic and continuing process. Even the Bible uses three tenses of the word—"I was saved, I am being saved, I will be saved." The Apostle Paul says, "Therefore, my dear friends, as you have always obeyed—not only in my presence, but now much more in my absence—continue to work out your salvation with fear and trembling" (Phil 2:12).

Traditionally Christianity affirms that hell is a real place for those who have not reconciled their sinful lives through faith in Christ. The New Testament speaks of hell as a place, the "lake of fire," into which, after the dead are raised, the unrighteous and even Hades are thrown. Jesus compared hell to "Gehenna," a public garbage dump outside Jerusalem where the wicked are sent. He used the term eleven times, describing it as a place of eternal punishment, even for hypocritical religious leaders of his time. Godless kings in the Old Testament, like Ahaz, were known to have sacrificed their children in this smoldering pit.

Others suggest that even if hell is real, it is likely a temporary place to pay for one's sins before moving up to a higher place of blessing. "Sheol" or "Hades" are different Bible words suggesting hell as the place of the dead, at least temporarily. The word "Purgatory" is used mostly in the Roman Catholic tradition as the place where souls go through purification. Those who ultimately do not repent are condemned to non-existence, while those who do bow at Christ's feet are allowed to enter God's eternal kingdom.

Liberal theology generally tends to reject the idea of an afterlife of punishment for one's sins, preferring a type of universalism, a belief that everyone ultimately is "saved" to be in God's presence. It dismisses the claim that hell is a real place that has eternal consequences. "How could a loving God send his creation to a place of eternal punishment?" they ask.

Except for those who believe that one's death is the final state, without any belief in an afterlife, it seems most people accept at a minimum that hell will be the complete absence of God's presence. To be so consumed with selfishness, greed, hate, lust, and hypocrisy with virtually no force of goodness, truth, righteousness, and love to confront self-deception is a type of hell. Even in the modern, secular world that focuses mostly on the "here and now," most people can at least recognize that evil can consume and destroy humans. One can literally live in "hell on earth."

The Unpardonable Sin

The biblical concept of blasphemy is known as the human action that cannot be forgiven by God. "And everyone who speaks a word against the Son of Man will be forgiven, but anyone who blasphemes against the Holy Spirit will not be forgiven" (Luke 12:10). While there is an array of misguided explanations as to what this sin actually is, the context seems clear that the blasphemy against the Holy Spirit is the attributing of works of the prince of demons to Jesus. Luke is saying that dishonoring the Son of Man is such a serious matter that total rejection of God by insinuating that his "holy" Spirit is "evil" is unforgiveable. Believing that the works of God are really from the Evil One is a wholesale denial of the one true God, manifested through His Son Christ Jesus, for which no remedy exists. Calling God evil and evil things God is a complete distortion of truth. One that lives in such a confused condition cannot find salvation because sin and evil have completely twisted their understanding of the Father, Son, and Holy Spirit.

An immediate reaction by most hearers is defense and even relief. "That is not me! I believe God exists and that Jesus is his Son. I know when I am wrong and even pray for forgiveness. I certainly don't blame God for things he did not do."

Justification of our lives and actions is a natural human response. Any comparison of any blasphemous condition may initially cause feelings of being judged. But in all honesty, it is possible that there could be some real distortion happening due to one's own sinfulness, especially compared to what is considered godly, right, and true by God's definitions. Remember that Jesus condemned the outwardly religious of his day as hypocrites and even as "a child of hell" (Matt 23:15). They certainly did not see themselves in those terms. In fact, only a few of the Pharisees acknowledged wrongs, though they sought to capture and kill Jesus at the same time.

Sin distorts our lives. Whether habitually lying, having an adulterous relationship, cheating on taxes, hating our enemies, abusing relationships, living a greedy life, or "playing religion," they are all actions which God does not want us to do because he loves us and wants the best for us. Each time we justify wrongs we diminish his will and purpose for our lives. Confession means agreeing with God that we fall short of the mark. Over time the cumulative effect of unrepentance twists and distorts our thinking and desires. In fact, the results of years of justification, blame, and avoidance literally change our view of reality and the true nature of God. What we once called wrong soon becomes "not so bad."

We then believe ourselves to be better than others and note to others the good things we have done. Often we categorize "big" sins and "little" sins, with a free pass for the ones deemed insignificant. Instead of wanting to be all God created us to be, we lower the bar to just "try to be good."

Wealth can be particularly treacherous. In the parable of the sower (Mark 4:1-20), Jesus taught about four kinds of soil where seeds were planted. Only the seeds planted in good soil flourish. Seeds planted on the hard path do not grow and are snapped up by the Evil One. Seeds planted in rocky ground are "rootless" and fall away with trouble and persecution. Those seeds sown among thorns hear the word, but the worries of this life and the deceitfulness of wealth and the desires for other things come in and choke the word, making it unfruitful. The sower, the symbol for God, wanted the seed to produce a bountiful harvest, up to one hundred times what was planted. Hard ground, rocky soil, and thorns all thwarted the results. While the seed planted among the thorns did have nutritious soil, "the worries of this life, the deceitfulness of wealth, and the desires for other things" choked out the crop. What the farmer wants is fruit in his garden. What God wants in us is "a fruitful life" that produces his will in the world.

Wealth is not necessarily evil. Without wealth wonderful things in God's world could not happen. The poor can be blessed by the rich to be able to buy food to feed their children, access shelters if they are homeless, and get medical care they could not otherwise afford. Donated money can help sustain nonprofits, bless church ministries, and fight public injustices. It is clear in the Bible that financial blessings are often a gift from God to be used for his kingdom. Condemning the rich because they have money is not God's goal, but guiding the way they use their financial gain as Christians is extremely important. "From everyone who has been given much, much will be demanded; and from the one who has been entrusted with much, much more will be asked" (Luke 12:48).

Wealthy people have additional burdens and worries because they are rich. God's desire is that they be good stewards of what has been given to them. Yet because wealth is deceitful and easily corrupts one's motives and purposes in life, the rich are constantly challenged with greed and overconsumption. Riches can tempt one to think that material blessings are directly tied to good works or God's favor, thus suggesting that those with less are more unworthy.

But I'm Not Rich!

Yes, you are. The global household median income is now at $10,000. The Pew Foundation determined by 2011 standards that only 13 percent of the world is considered "middle class," averaging daily income between $10.01 to $20.00. The poor live on $2 or less daily, the low income on $2.01 to 10.00/day, upper-middle income on $20.01 to $50, and high income on more than $50 a day, according to a Pew Research Center 2011 report.

Based on the Census Bureau, the median household income in 2016 in the United States was $59,149. The mean (average) household income set a new high of $83,143.

Ironically, at the same time one survey found that even with such large incomes by comparison, many who make six figure incomes feel poor. A survey showed that Americans believe it takes $150,000 a year to feel financially secure today, which is about three times the current median income (Rosenberg 2012). College debt, cost of living, retirement, healthcare, and other increases have many folks living paycheck to paycheck. Survey after survey shows many Americans would not consider themselves "rich" until they had a net worth of $5 million to $10 million. While earning $250,000 a year might not feel rich to those Americans, in reality they are in the 97th percentile nationwide, which means they earn more than 97 percent of all tax filers.

Because affluence is so subjective, being wealthy has become evaluated by comparison to one's peers. While most middle-class and upper-middle-class Americans may not feel wealthy, by most standards they are rich. If your household income is above $86,000, you are on the upper side of the percentage scale of income in the United States. "Net worth" has not been considered as a part of that number. By global standards, if one's income is more than $50 a day, they are considered wealthy.

Don't Judge Me

"For the time will come when people will not put up with sound doctrine. Instead, to suit their own desires, they will gather around them a great number of teachers to say what their itching ears want to hear" (2 Tim 4:3).

It is humanly natural that we want to associate with those who admire and recognize us, regardless of our choices. It is not uncommon for someone feeling the scorn of rejection by another to rebuke them with the words, "Don't judge me!" When we feel our choices and actions are disapproved by others, changing friends or lashing out are natural human tendencies. "It's my life and I can do whatever I want," they retort. And while true at one level, the essence of Christian faith disagrees.

Like a small child we blame others, make excuses, or avoid any response. Deep down, however, if there is any spirituality still alive, we know they are right. We were created by God to do his good will and glorify him forever. Choosing to become a Christian is choosing to give up one's life of self-rule by submitting to the rule of the Creator God who loves you and wants the best for you. While the decision may be a point in time decision, calling and serving Christ "Lord" is a lifetime of submitting to his Lordship. Each time we sin or "miss the mark," God's Spirit reminds and convicts us of the act of rebellion and our urge to return to self-rule. He also reminds us of the self-centered lifestyle that is more about "me" than the kingdom of God. While a non-Christian continues his or her independence from God may call the rebuke of friends to be "judgment," the Christian who is embedded in God's unconditional love calls it "conviction." The ongoing journey of the Christian is a life of hearing the Holy Spirit's loving convictions to be more conformed to the image of Christ.

Stages of Spiritual Development

Defensiveness is Stage One of a chaotic life, according to psychologist M. Scott Peck (Peck 1998, 187f). It is a self-absorbed worldview that is usually narcissistic, manipulative, lacking control, and disingenuous. Relationships do not matter, except for what they can do for the chaotic person themselves. Life centers around coercion, scapegoating, intellectual deviousness, lack of empathy, greed, and constant efforts to preserve an image of perfection. There are many persons that never emerge out of this selfish stage.

Even the religious get self-centered. Jesus told the parable of two men praying (Luke 18:9-14). The Pharisee stood and prayed about himself, saying, "God, I thank you that I am not like other men-robbers, evildoers, adulterers—even like this tax collector. I fast twice a week and give a tenth of all I get." Yet the tax collector nearby, who could not even look up at God, beat his chest in humility, praying, "God, have mercy on me, a sinner." Jesus was clear. Only the tax collector's prayer was heard. "For whoever exalts himself will be humbled, and he who humbles himself will be exalted," for like little children, the kingdom of God belongs to them (Luke 18:16).

However, as God's Spirit convicts of self-centeredness and reveals that there is more to life than such chaos, many come to learn about a loving God and experience conviction, confession, and a transforming faith that is new and exciting.

While many adults live out a whole life of childish, self-centered egotism, truth seekers move on to maturing stages of spiritual development. Stage Two most often emerges through understanding God through institutional Christianity and church life. For them church going, values, morals, attitudes, and habits of giving, praying, and service begin to replace their chaotic world and bring unknown joy in the new lifestyle with more order and relationships.

According to Peck, over time the structures of institutionalism begin to feel legalistic and rigid to those that are maturing. They often begin to wonder if there is more to their spiritual journey than rule following, often packaged as discipleship or spiritual steps. They have the courage to ask questions about "why we do it this way," followed by questions of doubt and uncertainty.

This third stage charts questioning and asking, "Why do we believe this?" Peck recognizes them as skeptics, individualists, questioners, and even doubters. Religious allegiance is replaced by a more logical base of truth that now wonders if other religions are legitimate or if God even exists. They reject strong, fundamentalist statements and often become ostracized by their former religious peers as becoming unspiritual. Having given up on the flawed institution, there are those who never move out of this stage and often leave the church.

The fourth stage in Peck's spiritual development model is when one begins moving away from the harshness and emptiness of the skeptic to see God as much more than the limited descriptions of the past institutional thinking as well as the doubter. In this stage maturity is now more about learning to listen, to love, and to share higher values. Becoming more contemplative and confessional like the psalmists, learning to worship deeply, becoming genuinely generous, learning to forgive and to reconcile broken relationships, and seeking God's shalom ("well-being") for the world are common traits. The truth seeker accepts the transcendence and mystery of God without having a rigid definition of these things. Heaven is understood as a joyous eternity in the presence of the loving Creator and Sustainer of life. Hell means everything outside his presence, where there is no love, no joy, no forgiveness, no hope, and no meaningful relationships. Jean-Paul Sartre's description of hell is an eternity of being in a "closed, windowless room" with other people who are dead to all things spiritual, lifeless, and self-serving forever and ever.

No longer bound by donations for tax purposes or name recognition, these mature Christians often give generously and silently to the needs of others. They consider their financial wealth as a privilege from God to invest in and care less and less about their own material gain.

How Hard It Is for the Rich to Enter the Kingdom of God

While it is still true that very few Christians enjoy being confronted, teachable followers of Jesus have the privilege to step back from any encounter and reflect on the truth of the loving rebuke or "judgment."

Whether from honest seeking or from a desire to receive yet another accolade as a wealthy and religious man, a rich young ruler approached the street rabbi who was drawing crowds wherever he went. The Teacher suggested there was just one more thing he needed to do. "Sell everything you have and give it to the poor, and you will have treasure in heaven. Then come follow me" (Matt 19:21).

As the wealthy young ruler walked away in sadness, Jesus said, "How hard it is for the rich to enter the kingdom of God." It is easier for a camel to squeeze through the "Needle Gate" in the Jerusalem Wall than for the wealthy to get into heaven.

Stunned by observing this encounter, the disciples said, "Who then can be saved?" With material blessings and religious obedience, we are all banished from the gates of heaven, they thought. With rapid appeal, Peter pled his case for all of them, "We have left all we had to follow you!" Indeed they had. The disciples had left their jobs, family, friends, homes, and any societal expectations to follow the Son of Man. Was the rich ruler supposed to do the same?

Discipleship is growing up in faith, just as Jesus pushed his own disciples to understand. He confronted James and John for their desire be first in the Kingdom by reminding them that the first are last and the last are first. He taught the disciples by example that washing their feet was God's way, not man's. He taught them in his prayer to the Father that forgiveness of others superseded being forgiven. His Sermon on the Mount in Matthew 5–7 was an unparalleled challenge to live righteously, love enemies, reject hate, lust, false oaths, worry about earthly treasures, and judging others. It even included a reminder to give to the needy without fanfare. Jesus touched lepers, sat with sinners, and confronted self-centered religious leaders. His judgment was based in love, even though the hard hearted could not see it and often defended their lifestyles. Discipleship always challenges us to change.

Give All You Can

John Wesley practiced what he preached. Known as the founder of Methodism in the eighteenth century, he and his brother, Charles, and George Whitefield engaged in disciplined ministry and out-door preaching to the unchurched. John is well known for his strong attitude toward upward financial mobility. His creed was, "Gain all you can; Save all you can; Give all you can." He preached and promoted "holy living," which encouraged earning more only to be able to give more away. Having grown up in poverty, he had learned to live simply, refusing to purchase unnecessary or extrav-agant things so he had more to share with others in need. While in Oxford, attending Lincoln University, he became convicted of his excessive spending and began living a life of discipline on a set income, thus increasing his generosity each year. He detested ex-pensive dining, fancy clothes, and luxurious furniture, all symbols of what could have been better spent on the poor. He even en-couraged parents not to purchase costly items for their children, therefore increasing their desires to spend money wisely.

A Guiding Moral Compass to Giving

While there are millions of wealthy Americans who give gen-erously to various causes, many donors operate more from im-pulse than purpose or priorities. When the church decides to build a new building or the urban youth needs a van, wealthy people often give, especially when there is a personal connec-tion to the cause. Unfortunately, a core approach to Aristotle's philosophy of the good life is often missed. He reasoned that one's values and virtues should direct philanthropic giving. One should make wise choices with practical judgment. Christian giving should be driven by ultimate, far-reaching goals. Wealthy people "have the capacity to produce alternatives to conditions and to set their hearts on great aspirations and responsibilities" (Schervish and Whitaker 2010, 7). These so-called hyperagents can make huge impacts on institutions and efforts which shape the material world. They are not just donors but the creators of charitable enterprises. In some ways acquiring wealth is easier than the required reflective thinking and discernment needed to make a difference in the world. "Discernment is a process of interior moral and spiritual dialogue in which discrete aspects of life are sifted through and ordered into meaningful patterns of purposeful decisions" (idem). Once these patterns have been established, the donor can move beyond the frequent appeals of fundraisers and causes to decide how he or she is called to make a more significant difference in God's world. Giving becomes more strategic and purposeful.

For example, in 2016 the Bill and Melinda Gates Foundation pledged $5 billion to health and anti-poverty initiatives in Africa. Their previous giving of $9 billion over the last fifteen years has already made a significant impact on the quality of life of some of the world's poorest people. According to the Philanthropy News Digest, "Gates has noted the progress African countries have made in reducing child mortality, eradicating polio, and fighting malaria and the HIV/AIDS epidemic and pointed to expanded access to contraceptives, the creation of new vaccines that protect children from pneumonia and severe diarrhea, and investments in strong, community-based primary healthcare systems in Malawi, Ethiopia, and Rwanda as additional signs of progress" (Philanthropy News Digest 2016). While few people have such enormous amounts of money to give, any philanthropist can target their financial blessings through clearly discerned intentions and make an impact on the issues that matter.

Spiritual transformation makes a radical change in the heart of a donor. Loving money is sinful, a "disgusting morbidity," but using money for one's "neighbor" is a high virtue. For the wealthy,

124

Commonwealth

developing a lifestyle that is somewhat indifferent to the lures of this world and focused on God's purposes is complicated and challenging. Yet the happiness of life, as Aristotle declares, will never be found in the myriad of daily activities and demands, but in actions that are directed by a reflective discernment and a virtuous heart. A moral compass integrates both personal capacity and the motives to make a difference. As more and more citizens become millionaires, the potential to literally change the world becomes possible. However, their desire to use their money for worthy purposes is grounded in their moral or spiritual biography founded on their fundamental goal in life. "They do not need to own more money, but to discern the moral compass that will guide the deployment of their wealth to enlarge this moral citizenship of care" (Schervish and Whitaker 2010, 9).

Hard Gets Harder for the Wealthy

"Again, I tell you, it is easier for a camel to go through the eye of a needle than for someone who is rich to enter the kingdom of God" (Matt 19:24). If his Sermon on the Mount was not overwhelming enough, Jesus implies that wealth makes it even harder. Like a large camel trying to enter the smaller nighttime gate into Jerusalem, entering the gate into God's kingdom appears to be even more difficult for the rich. A rich Christian who says they believe the Bible seems to have five choices. 1) Accept this hard saying and dig deeper into freedom from the enmeshment of wealth and faith in matters of salvation; 2) redefine wealth as blessings, not related to spiritual poverty; 3) discount the words of Jesus as out of touch with reality; 4) relegate his statements only for a particular person or situation, not a general teaching; or 5) assert that grace alone saves a sinner, and what he does with his money and possessions is secondary or unrelated to salvation.

In most cases we create a "cultural Christianity" that subtly blends how we live with what we like about the Bible, thus ignoring the hard sayings. While most Christians say they believe the Bible, studies suggest that statement is little more than lip service. Research by the Pew Foundation acknowledges that most Americans believe in a good God as Creator, Jesus as Savior, heaven and hell, and other general statements. Since no one wants to go to a burning fire and be outside the presence of a good God, "getting saved," baptized, being good, and joining a church is quite popular since many believe it leads to heaven. When questioned about what it means to be a Christian answers vary widely, ranging anywhere from "being good" to devoutly following Jesus' words and deeds. In more evangelical cultures, repeating the "sinner's prayer" seems to be enough to be forgiven and heaven-bound, while allowing the sinner to continue his lifestyle relatively unchanged. Church denominations have historically divided over the tension between grace and works as it relates to salvation.

Since one's possessions are usually embedded into his or her self-image, the high cost of sacrificing them seems inconceivable. Besides certain religious orders, such as certain Catholic and Orthodox ascetics as well as various cults, few mainstream or evangelical Christian traditions seem to seriously question the possibility that Jesus "really meant" what he said about the eternal implications of wealth.

Since it is the human tendency to justify our behavior and avoid the challenges of being transformed, it is very difficult for God's people to honestly seek the will of God. Genuine confession that acknowledges God's ways are not our ways requires courage to admit that the choices we have made and are making are not the best for our lives. More often we "baptize" our way of life. Like the compromised rich ruler who came to seek Jesus, we can become sad when our duplicity is exposed and we are commanded to "go sell all and follow."

Rarely do Christians today know anyone who has literally given up their possessions because of a deep desire to follow Christ. Perhaps they know the stories of St. Francis of Assisi, who abandoned a life of wealth, or Orthodox monks in medieval times who wandered the deserts and lived out a vow of poverty—but they were a special religious group, not business men and women living in the modern world. Some Christians have heard of various groups of Anabaptists from the Radical Reformation who often lived communally and simply, but to most American Christians they seemed more cultlike since they shared possessions and often separated themselves from the general society. Even today's "religious hipsters" may have been infatuated with a small evangelical Christian movement called "New Monasticism," encouraging simplicity and care for the poor in under-resourced urban neighborhoods around America. Yet these groups all seem like abnormal deviations to mainstream Christians who believe in God, confess their sins, have been baptized in church, read the Bible, and work hard to provide for their families, even while enjoying some of the benefits of their financial blessings. Surely God could not send people to hell just because they enjoyed the benefits of economic gain and a strong work ethic, especially if they occasionally gave offerings to the poor and marginalized in their own community. Or could he?

8

THE CHURCH IS BEING COOPTED

We, Not Me

"Many US Americans are prone to think that hyper-individualism, competition, and keeping oneself and our own national interests at the center of economic activities will lead us to the blessing of our nation. This is a false promise and hope" (Hinson-Hasty 2017, 214). Unfortunately, these self-centered views are deeply rooted in the local church in America and distort the very essence of what it means to be the church.

The early church did not have a rigid model on how to be the church—they just did what Jesus said to do. He told them to love God and their neighbors with all their heart, soul, and mind. He said to seek his kingdom before all else. He told them to forgive their enemies and do good to those who hurt them. He said be the light in dark places, give to the needy, not to worry about temporal things, do good deeds in secret, and not judge others. He told them not to hate, lust, or act piously. Not only did he say these things, he lived them. They watched Jesus deal with his religious accusers, feed a hungry crowd, touch lepers, heal the sick and oppressed, and sit at a well with an adulterous woman. They watched his deep-seated courage to say the truth at all costs, even though they mocked him, rejected him, put thorns on his head, and crucified him. He told his disciples to wait for the power of the Spirit to come before starting anything.

When the Spirit's power came, they did what was now natural to them, though supernatural to their culture. They unashamedly told the gospel of the Messiah who not only lived, died, and was resurrected, but who also conquered the last enemies of sin and death. People in the streets were transformed by the good news. Since many had come from distant places with no place to sleep, the Jesus followers invited them to stay in their homes. They ate together, learned from each other, prayed together, shared possessions, and were devoted to one another. Church happened and others wanted in.

When real church happens cities get changed. As the rag-tag followers hit the streets of Jerusalem they also healed the sick, fed the hungry, cared for the blind, lame, and mentally ill. With courage and faith they shared their time, possessions, and authority over evil. And the church grew.

Centuries later historians noted, "The early Christians revitalized life in Greco-Roman cities by providing new norms and new kinds of social relationships that enabled them to cope with many urgent urban problems. They offered an immediate basis for attachment and brought a new and expanded view of family to society that was filled with the homeless and impoverished, and widows and orphans. In this sense, the early Christians provided a new basis for social solidarity" (Inoue 2017, 13).

What Happened?

The Western church is struggling. It is not only diminishing in numbers but in impact on its own culture. A growing postmodern secularism has produced a rising number of millennials called "nones," consisting of one-third of Americans who have opted out of religion in general and Christianity in particular. According to Wesley Granberg-Michaelson, former General Secretary of the Reformed Church in America, "White U.S. congregations are withering. From 1991 to 2014, the number of white Protestants declined by a third, a trend that will continue as they age: Though 20 percent of Americans are 18 to 34 years of age, only 1 in 10 white Protestant congregations reflects that in their attendance. As a result, more than half of U.S. congregations now have fewer than 100 members. Hundreds will close this year" (Granberg-Michaelson 2019).

Ironically, global Christianity in Africa and the global South continues to grow, while the only significant church growth in the West is among multiracial and Pentecostal churches. Many of these nontraditional, charismatic congregations are committed to empowerment and social transformation in their own communities, while American Christianity has been labeled as a gospel that was coopted by American power and wealth. Various studies now estimate that a quarter of Americans do not attend any church service, including both Protestants and Catholics. Over one half of Americans attend only a few times (Pew Foundation 2019). However, even while attendance declines, most Americans still consider religion, including Christianity, as positive for America. "Fifty-five percent say churches and religious organizations do more good than harm in society (compared with 20 percent of people who think it does more harm than good)" (Bailey 2019).

Authentic Religion

A common theme heard by younger millennials who are leaving the church is that they are tired of the "talk without the walk." In their eyes the church has become impotent and inconsistent with its stated values to serve and love others. Examples of sexual misconduct among the clergy, rejection of changing sexual values, lack of racial diversity, political syncretism, and inadequate engagement in one's local community have contributed to their judgment. They tend to believe that they can find "spirituality" outside organized religion, picking and choosing different options, usually with lower standards of expectations than weekly attendance in a church. While some of these young adults still admittedly long for transcendence and relationships, many have dismissed the church's ability to deliver genuine guidance without a set of rules with which they do not necessarily agree. "Nones" often see and hail Jesus as a legitimate renegade who rejected the outward religion of his day, but know little of the love that drove his mission.

The essence of the gospel is to love God and others with all our hearts. The essence of the church is to be the people of God who live out his call as a community of faith in a social context. The reality seems to be that we are not seeking those priorities. At best there are still some churches who acknowledge these goals, but others have simply given up being the visible Body of Christ that is the "salt, light and yeast" that changes its culture to be conformed to the image of Christ.

There are numerous reasons the church in the West is struggling, and no quick fixes will help. It seems that there are at least three factors that must be considered to enact meaningful change in their own communities.

First, long-lasting intimate relationships have been impacted by divorce and mobility, where family and friendship allegiance are now more marginalized in the culture by individualism. Though most everyone has a deep desire to be loved and even to love another, to be known and loved intimately feels threatening. Living alone in a big city, attending a crowded concert, and even "going to church" rarely offer genuine opportunities to be truly known. Many have never been involved in or witnessed a church that functions well in their "one-another" interactions. To be with those Christians who love one another, bear one another's burdens, encourage one another, and serve one another dispels fears and misperceptions of the essence of church for those who are searching.

Second, we seem less reflective about life. While definitions vary, individualist cultures tend to see people through the lens of autonomous, self-directed persons who deeply value independence, contrasted with more collective cultures that see people as connected and embedded in their social context. Friends often become more revered than family or a local community. Although humans have the capacity to exist at some level in

both spheres, Western culture has morphed toward individualism more than other cultures, although each year more nations
become individual-centric. Because of education and wealth,
leaving the nuclear family to discover one's interests and dreams
in the broader context changed the fabric of society. It has also
changed particular collectives which once attracted people. For
example, as a young adult I was invited by a men's civic club to
join them as a member. We met weekly, raised funds for worthy
causes, and took great pride in our national affiliation. This organization no longer exists in the same community where it once
thrived. While some collectives have survived, many struggle to
grow at all. Associations have diminished in value, especially to
the growing postmodern culture.

Third, a deep sense of purpose (*telos*) is lacking. When the
day is done, most everyone longs to be a part of something
that has authentic value, however that may be defined. While
occasional volunteerism may temporarily soothe the emptiness of a self-centered life, it does not fulfill the soul. On the
other hand, engagement against social injustices, empowering the poor, raising funds over time for a special need, or
advocating for a worthy cause move in the right direction. "A
strong telos protects against selfishness, cynicism, and dis-
trust. It allows for robust inquiry and free individual action.
It lends meaning to struggle and pain, fostering individual
grit and interdependence" (Snyder 2019, 99).

When all three of these converge, real life begins to happen at
a deeper level for the person searching for more. Deepening relationships for a common cause over an extended period of time
creates an environment that can be both positively self-centered
and more selfless and others-focused at the same time.

Christian Community Development

"Poverty is fundamentally relational and its cause is fundamentally
spiritual" (Meyers 1999, 13). At a holistic level, we must assume that
the negative and oppressive forces that work against the poor's well
being have a spiritual root. God made all of creation "good," and

hungry children are not in his will. While many churches tend to "blame the victim" for their poverty, it is more often the corrupt and dysfunctional structures and forces that dictate escape from their harsh realities. Powerless people need physical, mental, and spiritual empowerment to become more of who God created them to be. Only God can ultimately "make all things new." Transformation comes as Christ is allowed to be Lord over all our lives and social structures. It is not simple and easy, but in a self-serving, sinful world God's power through his people is the only way to bring sinful structures down.

The kingdom of God is not about checking things off a list of things to do for God, but forming and developing a loving relationship with him and our neighbors. According to Jesus, the first and second commandments are intrinsically integrated. "Hearing that Jesus had silenced the Sadducees, the Pharisees got together. One of them, an expert in the law, tested him with this question: 'Teacher, which is the greatest commandment in the Law?' Jesus replied: 'Love the Lord your God with all your heart and with all your soul and with all your mind.' This is the first and greatest commandment. And the second is like it: 'Love your neighbor as yourself.' All the Law and the Prophets hang on these two commandments'" (Matt 22:34-40).

When Helping Hurts

Unfortunately, misguided methods of helping the poor have often caused unintended harm to the poor. One of the most well-read books about poverty alleviation, called *When Helping Hurts: How to Alleviate Poverty without Hurting the Poor and Yourself* by Steve Corbett and Brian Fikkert has been printed in five languages and sold over 300,000 copies. In the book they suggest that seeing the single cause of poverty as a lack of resources or a lack of education, or a lack of knowledge, or oppression by powerful people tend to oversimplify the resolve. Based on some of the work of Bryant Meyers and his ministry at World Vision, they propose that poverty is relational, as in relation to God, self, others, and creation as a whole. There are three primary stages of need in the life of the poor: relief, reha-bilitation, and development. "One of the biggest mistakes that North American churches make, by far, is in applying relief in situations when rehabilitation or development is the appropriate intervention" (101). So many Americans see poverty as a lack of material resources and think giving money or possessions will change the condition of the recipient. Rarely is that the case. "As someone who studies poverty solutions and social and health inequalities, I am convinced by the academic literature that the biggest reason for poverty is how a society is structured. With-out structural changes, it may be very difficult if not impossible to eliminate disparities and poverty" (Assar 2017).

Jesus went a step farther: "I no longer call you servants, be-cause a servant does not know his master's business. Instead, I have called you friends, for everything that I learned from my Father I have made known to you," and so he upended the social structures of traditional culture (John 15:15). Jesus dismissed the traditions of man that created social categories of the "haves and have nots." There really is no "rich and poor" in the kingdom of God, only family members and friends. Our joy is made complete only when we love each other, even to the point of giving one's life away for them. The call to the rich is not to give more money, but to become friends with those who have no money. It means ending qualifiers like "deserving" and "undeserving" poor, and replacing those terms of judgment with, mostly simply, "friend."

The biblical connection between one's salvation and one's ethics cannot be ignored. They are holistically intertwined. The Apostle Paul clearly recognized that complete renunciation of everything owned is not enough to birth someone into God's kingdom. "If I give all I possess to the poor and surrender my body to the flames, but have not love, I am nothing" (1 Cor 13:3). Loving others with the love of Christ, particularly the poor, comes from an internal transformation demanding an external manifestation. "If anyone has material possessions and sees his brother in need but has no pity on him, how can the love of God be in him?" (1 John 3:17). Biblically it is inconceivable that a

Christian can be in a covenant with God and ignore the needs of men and women. "We know we have passed from death to life, because we love our brothers. Anyone who does not love remains in death" (1 John 3:14). The sin of the rich young ruler was not his wealth alone, but the observation of Jesus that he could not see the needs of the poor and share his wealth. Entering the kingdom of heaven is not about divestment. "The internal nature of salvation demands cultivating pure and passionless souls with God's help, not getting rid of external goods and possessions" (Rhee 2012, 79). It is through lifelong discipleship and discipline that the follower of Christ understands spiritual poverty and humility as the building blocks of maturity. Once the believer has overcome the entrapment of possessions, power, and prestige, he or she finds extreme joy and privilege to sacrificially share physical needs with those who are in need. Yet more than individual works of righteousness for others, the greater context is in Christian community with "brothers and sisters" who collectively share their possessions and address injustice both locally and globally.

Our Money Follows Our Hearts

I live in a convoluted job. What began with Janet and me as a full time "hands-on" ministry among the poor and marginalized almost three decades ago eventually grew into a ministry with eighty staff members, fifteen buildings, and over twenty programs. We never intended to be a large nonprofit organization with a $4 million-dollar budget. Janet and I just kept doing the next thing as we continuously encountered unmet human needs in our community.

Job responsibilities morphed with that kind of organic growth. Going from playing basketball with urban kids on the court at my house to becoming president and executive director pushed the limits of my skill set each step of the way. Hiring qualified, Christian staff to oversee and develop programs for urban children and youth, the homeless, addicted, unemployed, sick, mentally ill, and abused were critical. Finding adequate vol-

unteers and training them to understand our model of empowerment took time. Building an infrastructure to sustain it all was
even more challenging. From maintaining a healthy board of
directors to overseeing the craziness, we had budgets, financial
audits, legal responsibilities, newsletters, speaking engagements,
transportation expectations, staff training, and building maintenance issues. Our growth now included just under one hundred
toilets to keep flushing!

At each stage of growth financial obligations increased. What
began from support from our own checkbook and a few donations from friends who believed in us was growing way beyond our personal abilities to support. After the initial grant a
few years later from Christian Mission Concerns, there was a
baseline of support that sustained Mission Waco. However, it
was obvious we had to build a larger donor base from the community if we were to grow and maintain our programs to serve
others. While telling the stories of those we served to churches, civic clubs, and others was (and is) our primary approach
to fundraising, we also began to have local events. An annual
banquet with a guest speaker who acknowledged our ministry's
approach, complemented by volunteer recognitions, a talented
presentation of our urban children performing a ballet dance,
kids playing musical instruments, and still others acting out a
brief theater piece, helped those in attendance understand the
value of supporting our ministry in the community. Yet there
was more need. In time we created an annual golf scramble, a
style show, a sports breakfast, and a neighborhood race to help
underwrite the budget. Through the leadership of our capable
staff these events not only helped build our ministry, but also engaged local citizens to learn about Mission Waco Mission World.

Scandals have always beleaguered nonprofit organizations.
Passionate appeals from hunger alleviation groups, war veteran
organizations, disease researchers, and numerous "do-good"
agencies have usually been successful methods, especially with
mass media tools. Unfortunately, through the years several
well-known nonprofits and churches have been exposed for

improper use of the donations they received. Whether improper use of funds, poor internal management, or outright theft, these exposures have deeply hurt the majority of organizations that have done everything right. The result of those news stories in the public forum have caused many donors who once gave to mistrust most nonprofits.

In the last several years, one significant positive response to thwart mismanagement activities has been a growing legal requirement for public disclosure by the IRS and the States from which tax-exempt nonprofits do business. In general, nonprofits, excluding churches, which normally receive $25,000 or more in annual income must file 990s and Schedule A. All nonprofits with $100K in annual contributions or over $250K in assets are required to file an IRS Form 990. This public disclosure has provided a way for the public, including interested donors, to evaluate the finances of the nonprofit organizations they want to support. Long before such requirements were mandated, Mission Waco accepted the biblical challenge that everything we do should be "above reproach." While the cost of outside audits and annual financial accountability can be challenging, we believe our public exposure should be a testimony of our faith. As a result, Charity Navigator, the largest evaluator of nonprofits in America, has awarded Mission Waco Mission World with their highest four-star charity designation for six of the last seven years. The most recent rating was an overall rating of 97.26 points out of a perfect 100 points (96.13 for financial; 100 for transparency and accountability). Only 19 percent of all the charities they evaluate receive this four-star rating for four years, as we have, "verifying that Mission Waco Mission World exceeds industry standards and outperforms most charities in America. It sets you apart from its peers and demonstrates public trustworthiness" (Thatcher 2019).

Impulse and Holiday Generosity

In reality, donations to churches and Christian nonprofit organizations are not nearly as impacted by irresponsible donors as they are by certain donors' inconsistent and seasonal giving patterns.

For obvious reasons consistent donations are the lifeblood of these organizations. Creating a ministry budget to serve others is challenging without patterns of giving to rely on. Unfortunately, approximately 30 percent of annual ministry or church budgets are not given until the last six weeks of the fiscal year. Even then we discover that many donors randomly select recipients, giving to one organization this year and a different one the next year. Holidays and year-end tax write-offs amplify the focus of donors. The challenge is that relatively small amounts are donated in summer months, when the poor are still in need and many of their children cannot access school lunches. Utility bills are usually higher and charities rarely have enough funds to help.

A People of Power

While community organizing has impact, it is now "increasingly recognized that society could not be significantly changed unless both workers and management, both poor and middle-class, both inner-city and suburbanite, red and yellow, black and white shared in building power together. And that power has to be built relationally-by discovering our common issues and pains, and by caring what happened to each other" (Linthicum 2006, 12). Unlike community organizing, broad-based organizations and institutions must be built to set free the oppressed. The "shalom communities" are people of well being and care how God's resources are used for physical safety, affordable housing, adequate jobs, healthcare, environmental friendliness, and living in peace (Linthicum 2006, 22).

Personal and Corporate Philanthropy Trends

The headline of our local paper read, "Americans giving less and less: Local nonprofits and charities hurting" (*Waco Tribune-Herald* 2019). With so many billionaires today and exorbitant business deals announced daily, how could that be? It is no secret that most of the wealth in America is owned by a very small percentage of the population. "Because of rising inequality throughout the economy, the very wealthy have amassed enormous stockpiles of treasure, leaving little for everyone else" (Ingraham 2019). Most of the rich today are baby boomers "who collectively own 21 percent of the nation's wealth," much of which will not flow down to Generation X'ers or millennials. In fact, some economists believe that the financial hole that today's younger generation experience will increase compared to their parents.

While millennials have become the largest demographic in the American workforce, this generation is changing philanthropy patterns. Some analysts note that a higher percent of them donate than other generations, yet how they give and to whom they give seems to be changing. With smart phones and internet peer-to-peer appeals, many do not employ monthly bank withdrawals to specific charities or planned giving donations, but are motivated by specific issues that may move them to make a one-time gift. Crowdfunding, emotional stories, disaster relief, and other urgent appeals are frequently the driving forces that initiate charity. Many millennials also consider volunteerism as philanthropy, softening the demand of direct appeals for funds.

While middle-class income is shrinking, the poor in the United States are now confronted with a growing lack of affordable housing, low wages, and a lack of health care. Homeless camps have continued to grow throughout the nation as rents spike too high for the average worker to sustain.

Many wealthy Americans have assuaged any feelings regarding their overabundance through generous donations to nonprofit organizations, churches, and special needs such as disaster relief, higher education, and environmental concerns. In fact, $410 billion was given in 2017, according to Giving USA 2018, amounting to approximately 2.1 percent of the GDP. While that amount was an increase of $20 billion from the previous year, the middle class donated less that year. According to the Lilly Foundation, "the share of Americans who give money to charity fell from about 68.5% in 2002 to 53.1% in 2016, the most recent year for which data is available" (Ware 2018). The increase of actual funds came from fewer households who gave about $500 more, about $2,514 in 2014. Yet even with a strong economy, changes in the national tax laws now worry charities, which depend significantly on individual donations. These changing trends are concerning, especially since community-based charities meet significant needs of the poor and marginalized that are not met elsewhere. Unlike former fundraising campaigns built around themes like "Everybody gives, everybody benefits," the norm seems to now be, "Fewer give, fewer benefit."

Church Donation Trends

Historically as much as one third of all donations in America are given to churches and religious purposes. But church donations and religious-based giving are now shrinking. Giving USA reports that "in 2018, gifts to religious organizations are down 1.5 percent to just 29 percent of total charitable giving." On average, Americans gave away only 1.9 percent of their disposable income to any group, and churches are included in this trend. Americans gave about 3 percent of their disposable income to churches in 1968, and less than 2.2 percent in 2016.

Lack of discretionary income is one reason, yet there are other reasons. Lower attendance in churches adds to the dilemma. A study by Lifeway Research found that six in ten Protestant churches had plateaued or declined in attendance in the past twelve months and more than half saw fewer than ten people become new Christians. While growth tended to increase among larger churches of 250 members or more, donations have declined in small churches of fifty members or less. Pentecostal churches are growing significantly more that evangelical and mainstream congregations.

Generational mindsets also affect giving. In the past, boomers were usually more loyal to the "organization" than to specific purposes that the church sought to do. Millennials, however, generally do the opposite. Reasons for this include an avoidance of biblical teaching about giving for fear of overreaction from attendees who believe "churches are always asking for money." Church health is also a factor, particularly in the Roman Catholic Church, which has experienced significant decline in donations due to their sexual abuse scandal. The impact of this giving trend to institutional churches is still unknown, especially with the growth of "nones." Many of these postmodern thinkers have simply written off the American church as irrelevant.

The international impact of the COVID-19 pandemic on generosity to churches and nonprofits is still unknown in the big picture, but trends have already suggested a downward curve on donations. With a potential longer-term recession, the tension between holding on to one's assets or giving to causes for the poor has increased the dilemma of how we use the wealth God has given us. The nest egg of so many who put their faith in an ever-increasing stock market has led to panic for those whose wealth was their security. Even as the poor sink deeper into survivalism, the temptation of the rich and middle class is to hold on to what one has for a "rainy day" or retirement. More than ever, Christians will need to put their trust in God, not mammon.

Back to the Future . . . of the Church

Some would argue that the reality of church and denominational decline could be a good thing. The ebb and flow of history might concur. What were once the hallmarks of the early Church have diminished in many ways. The first followers of Jesus were just ordinary men and women who watched their leader live out genuine love, sacrifice, and compassion. Being filled with his power and example, they emulated his lifestyle in their cities and, because of this, the world has been impacted.

At its core, Christian community development is Christian. While there are important principles that can be used across development models of change, there are core values that are untenable outside this one. Doing good for urban folks matters and is worthy of one's time. However, being sent in the name of Christ and empowered by his Spirit embraces a different dimension of helping. It acknowledges that humans were created in the image of God. It affirms that the church is God's body on earth that he uses to bring healing in multiple dimensions. It recognizes that the helper, as well as the helped, are both sinners in a sinful world and share a common grace from God. It acknowledges that hope, faith, and love remain, "the greatest of which is love" (1 Cor 13:13).

9

POVERTY OF SPIRIT IS THE BEGINNING

Awakening from an Illusion

In "grey town" it rains forever outside the walls and even inside their dwellings. C. S. Lewis' imaginative allegory of hell in *The Great Divorce* describes a skyward bus ride to an unknown location away from the city. Even as the limited number of those eligible who personally choose to enter the journey break through the rain and clouds into the beautiful sunshine, their distorted presuppositions and negative attitudes distort the reality of what is really happening. Most of the bus riders are so entrenched in their illusions of the purpose of life that they cannot understand the evolving and glorious journey toward heaven. They wish they had never left "grey town," giving various justifications for choosing the joyless, friendless, and futile lives of their pasts, instead of risking the unknown of what could be. As it turns out, the bus riders never realized they were heaven-bound to a place where joy is normal. They could not see through the clouds of their own presuppositions and tainted views that what they deeply wanted was blurred by misunderstanding and lack of trust. Their rejection of the unknown was coopted by their fears and lust to return to former safe places in grey town, which was hell itself. Even some who continued on the bus were damned from the final heavenly destination, which required turning away from their cherished evils. The good news is that those bus riders who continued to honestly seek understanding and acknowledge their sins as they were revealed found the kingdom of God.

Transformation is a holistic process recognized by practical changes, new insights, clear direction, and character development. There are no quick steps or shortcuts. Without conviction and a genuine desire to change, few people actually do. More often defensiveness, avoidance, and redirection, a type of "yes/but" rhetoric, continue to frame one's illusory beliefs. Many are like those in "grey town" who, despite enlightenment and its implications, prefer to continue believing what they formerly did and miss the joy presented to them. In Lewis' allegory the "solid people" purposely approach individual ghosts to encourage them to stay and travel to the mountains with them toward a glorious destination. They encourage the ghosts to stick it out, certain that they will get acclimated to this new world and eventually grow solid themselves, especially if they abandon their petty problems. Unfortunately, the narrator overhears many such conversations as the ghosts, one by one, give up their journey toward truth.

Change involves faith, believing what is right and true but not yet actualized. It takes steps toward the revealed truth and challenges those who follow to lay down their old presuppositions for the new. It also involves concern for the wellbeing of others. "In Matthew's view, Christians find their true identity when they are involved in mission, in communicating to others a new way of life, a new interpretation of reality and of God, and in committing themselves to the liberation and salvation of others" (Bosch 2014, 84). God's Spirit is always on time for those who are seeking and wanting more in life. Often the awakening surprises and even brings fear to people as they examine the cost of change. Whether from a life crisis or a time of questioning oneself, there are those moments when God seems to break into the chaos of one's self-centered life with a call to a more meaningful existence. Conversion into a life outside self-absorption and institutionalized ritual means risk and faith. There is often a time of thinking outside the institutional walls of societal expectations that leaves more room for questioning and even healthy doubt. If the spiritual sojourner ultimately becomes a truth seeker, hungry to understand and follow the path of God's kingdom, there is a new joy that emerges regardless of the challenges of change ahead. Each step brings deeper insights and meaning in life. The long-sought fruits of joy, purpose, love, reconciliation, and goodness that money could never buy now become the by-products of simple faith. There is a deep peace that allows one to accept those who disagree or whose lifestyles are different, and yet a genuine compassion about how to help them become all God created them to be.

In the midst of spiritual transformation, questioning one's own motivation and actions becomes normative. Even those who are wealthy and entangled in a quest for more become free to examine what really matters and why they have such a need for approval and a desire for the icons of luxury. Who cares how many expensive cars are driven or signature golf courses are played? How many pairs of shoes and expensive clothes does one really need, especially in the presence of the naked and shoeless ones who now can be seen? Serving others gradually becomes a new way of life. News reports from around the world about those experiencing famine of floods or persecution now are newsworthy because of the suffering of fellow brothers and sisters. Even in the confusion voiced by family and friends about these attitudinal and behavioral changes, there is a deep and unwavering solace that life is now full of meaning and purpose. Now there is no going back. Each step of faith strengthens the desire to move forward in yet another step.

Poverty Simulation

For many this journey into "zoe," a life full of purpose, comes through natural experiences. In our case, buying a home in a blighted neighborhood dramatically changed our family's life.

Looking back over the last forty-three years in the same house that was once filled with rats and roaches on crime-ridden streets, we discovered it was the best decision we ever made. Without the luxury of middle-class culture, we began to see outside our own small world. The blessings far outweighed the challenges and the joy of a life we discovered could not be compared to a good day on the stock market or a triumphant sports event. While we were uncertain of the road ahead, we were certain that God would be faithful and good and lead us deeper into his kingdom.

Several months after moving into the house, a youth pastor from a respected white, middle-class church in Oklahoma City called to ask for our help. Although his growing youth group attended Bible studies and worship services regularly, it was obvious to him that his teens were failing to confront the powerful challenges of Jesus revealed in their Bible discussions to change their lifestyles. Instead of enacting change, these truths were coopted by their own environment. Unlike the Lord's example of loving the poor, caring for the "half-breed" Samaritans, and even touching lepers, these students justified their racial prejudice, had little tolerance for the poor, and blamed those who struggle in America for their own suffering.

His experience was similar to what many pastors and Christian educators often discover, regardless of how well rehearsed their Sunday sermon or Bible lesson. Culture, especially affluent culture, tends to shape the lifestyles of most Christians more than religious indoctrination and shallow prayer. The gap between orthodoxy (right doctrine) and orthopraxy (right actions) seems to grow wider and wider. Instead of struggling with the deep truths of the Bible, enculturation affords many church attendees an avenue to blend and justify the prophetic message of Jesus into a self-serving defense of motives and ethics that best suits one's preferred choices. Bible verses are even quoted out of context to defend oneself, even when it is clear that the message and actions of Jesus cannot support this twisted thinking. Like the religious Pharisees of Jesus' time, the Law has been distorted to defend godless actions.

To help the youth pastor, we agreed to organize a poverty simulation that would focus more on the challenges of being poor than on long discussions about poverty. To make it applicable, each youth and sponsor who attended was asked to keep only four items they brought with them, turn in all their money, watches, jewelry, and phones, then exchange the clothes they were wearing with the thrift store clothes made available for the weekend. Each participant was subsequently given the equivalent "play money," symbolizing the real amount of funds a mom with three children receives on welfare for a similar amount of time. From Friday evening until Sunday afternoon, each participant had to pay with their own "welfare money" for everything they received. Housing, food, showers, and other basics had a nonnegotiable price tag. From sleeping on the ground, sporadic meals, and long periods of walking, the sheer physical demands exhausted them. Added to these were several other experiences such as deep discussions and times of reflection. The unpredicted rain only increased their torment. The sharing time on Sunday afternoon was remarkable. Students confessed their closed-mindedness about the poor, prejudice toward people of color, and even their *noblesse oblige* (privilege) as a right. A few shared Bible verses that finally had real meaning to them. There was prayer, the real kind, and even a few tears. In forty-two hours, God's Spirit had awakened the deadness of their souls to see and hear.

What started as single weekend exploded into a life-changing impact for thousands. Over twenty-five thousand participants have now gone through the Mission Waco poverty simulation that is offered about twelve times a year. Most of the participants have similar awakenings. Our privilege has been to hear the stories of transformation from so many who continued their journeys of learning, sacrifice, and service to the poor and marginalized throughout these thirty years. Others became prophetic when they returned home and shared with their parents, pastors, and friends about their conviction to change many of their self-indulgent behaviors. Now they sponsor impoverished children in other countries to attend school, go to serve in low-income housing complexes in their own communities, buy water wells in villages where drinking from bacteria-laden rivers is normative, and help urban children improve their reading skills.

Due to a widening interest in this transformative weekend, Janet and I wrote a book called *Plunge2Poverty* that helped others from around the nation understand the principles behind the model, the activities that are important, and the "do's and don'ts" that protect the impact of the weekend. Over the years, two different television crews from France have come to do stories on the Poverty Simulation to share insights with their viewers about how some American Christians understand poverty and train others to combat it.

Even Millionaires Came

The phone call was a bit unusual. A father of one of the former participants in the poverty simulation wanted to know more about the experience his daughter had in Waco. At first it seemed like he was suspicious, but as we talked it was clear that his reason for calling was to understand the change in her. When she returned home, his daughter seemed to have a different attitude about life. She had seen the pictures, heard the stories, and even felt some of the realities that poor people experience day in and day out. For a few days, she even chose not to sleep in her plush bed, choosing instead to sleep on the floor. Through the weeks she seemed to appreciate her blessings and was concerned for those who were materially poor.

He then explained the backstory. He and his wife were millionaires who were living the life of luxury. Even as professing Christians who did seem to care for others, he acknowledged they wanted more in life. "I am part of an international organization called YPO, The Young Presidents' Organization. We pride ourselves in being a premier leadership organization composed of top executives from all over the world that seek to impact communities, business practices, and personal development. Some of us are Christians and some are not, but we are all wealthy and committed to empowerment for professionals across a variety of industries and regions. Would you allow our organization and family members to experience your poverty simulation?"

The weekend was arranged and twenty-seven of them came for the forty-two-hour experience, fully embracing the training. Because the poor have little power over their own circumstances, Mission Waco did not provide details about the weekend, only that they would be "poor." The mere mystery of not being in control was hard enough for these wealthy leaders. As the weekend progressed other components of the training opened up deep discussions and insights into their lives.

By Sunday afternoon God had done some great work in their lives, including some reevaluation of values and fears, and a desire to become more compassionate in both relationships and giving. Some of them decided to support extremely poor children to go to school in Haiti. Others committed to pay for water wells in developing countries. Still others chose to become involved in our microloan programs for poor women. While their takeaways varied, there was similarity in hearts. For one full weekend, those who lived in plenty had seen the world through the eyes of those who had little. With this group experience, their subsequent conversations back home had fresh insights when they gathered. They had the courage to ask how those insights changed them and what the implications going forward would be.

Experiences such as the poverty simulation can be a significant catalyst in the transformative process of the wealthy, where normal daily encounters with the poor become opportunities for real change. Position, power, and riches can have an increasingly corrosive impact on the affluent that slowly diminish their sensitivity and efforts to seriously engage with the poor and marginalized. Writing a large check to a nonprofit organization, playing in their golf scramble fundraiser, or participating in an art auction, while important, do not get to the

core of the problem. Even church attendance, a turkey dinner
donation to the homeless shelter, or meal time prayers which
"bless the poor" can be noble actions, but certainly do not have
the awakening impact similar to the rich young ruler or Zacchaeus. It often takes a significant encounter with God's Spirit
in a unique and extended environment, like an "exposure trip"
to a developing country, to discover years of false justification
and unrealized good intentions toward the poor and marginalized. In some cases, awareness of one's superficial lifestyles
serving mammon may come from critical situations such as a
heart attack, a divorce, or bankruptcy. In the darkness of those
experiences God reminds us all that there is so much more to
life than another deal or pleasure trip. We are awakened to the
brevity of life and see how much time is wasted chasing those
things that ultimately do not matter.

Get Honest in Your Own Garden

It's hard to get honest, real honest, even vulnerable. Self-deceit is
deep. There is something in our human psyche that short-circuits
personal conviction and calls for change that might disrupt who
we have become and who we are called to be. Just as Adam and
Eve hid from God after they disobeyed, and his unconditional
love gave them opportunity to still be seen and accepted for who
they were and how they acted. Excuses, justification, and blame
for their actions were inadequate to God. Only confession and
repentance could refresh the God-man relationship and restore
the intimate connections that the Creator intended for all of his
creation.

We often fear being known at the deepest level. Our human
need is to share our successes, titles, and reasons we have become who we are, hiding the lies and deception of personal
compromise, moral failure, and ignored convictions. The sad-
dest part is that we often begin to believe those very lies. "I didn't
know," "I thought you meant," "She made me." The empty words
desperately seek cover instead of raw confession. "I was wrong,"
"I disobeyed," "I was deceived," "Forgive me."

What God intended as life in the Garden of Eden is disrupted outside of it. Once outside his intimate presence, brokenness expands and the world's influence grows. As with Adam and Eve, the ground gets hard. There is pain in childbirth. Brother kills brother. Wars against those who disagree increase. Slavery, power, poverty, and hunger are the new reality. And all that the Creator intended for good seems lost in the abyss of self-centeredness that exists outside the Garden of intimacy with God.

Pain becomes a part of life, even when the reasons for it are not clear. Just ask Job, a servant of God who suffered from plentiful pain and suffering. He lost his income, his family, his house, his status in the community, and even his health. "What did you do wrong?" Job's wife asks. Her quick fix to the cesspool of pain was to "curse God and die" (Job 2:9). Many of God's children seek to end their suffering by checking out physically, mentally, and emotionally. It often seems to be the easiest way, especially if we believe that our human condition cannot be reversed. Job remarkably responds in the midst of horrible pain, "yet I will praise him" (Job 13:15). He chose life even though most all of the temporal blessings that matter to humankind had evaporated like a morning fog. Stripped of everything that had earthly value, Job's confidence was in the same Creator God who offered us a garden and a relationship.

Sometimes being honest only comes when we are stripped naked of the shallow and temporal things we wear. While our own journeys are different and unique, ultimately they are the same. Rich or poor, black, white or brown, kings or slaves, we each stand naked in front of the God of the garden who sees each of us as we really are. We can ignore him, make excuses, promise to return to him "at a later date," or even curse God and die. The alternative choice is to stand naked and vulnerable before the God of the garden and admit who we really are. In those moments we can choose to enter life more fully than ever before and accept the invitation to "become" what God created us to be.

Trusting with Childlike Faith

Once the courage to be honest and see oneself as God sees us occurs, the journey deepens. Seeing God more clearly requires simple faith. Trusting him often costs us. The youngest of the four siblings in the Pevensie home, Lucy is a fictional character in C. S. Lewis' acclaimed book, *The Lion, the Witch and the Wardrobe*, a part of the Chronicles of Narnia series. After discovering a doorway in the back of a wardrobe, Lucy and the other children are transported into an imaginary world of animals, witches, and the formidable Aslan. Their escapades reveal both the undeterred faith of Lucy to see what the other siblings cannot see nor understand. Her simple, childlike faith rejects their jokes and cynicism, ultimately winning them over to see Aslan, the mighty lion whose love for those in his kingdom never dies. After the lion's death at the Stone Table, the intimate relationship that Lucy and her sister Susan experienced with Aslan help the brothers to see what they formerly could not see. With new eyes and new courage, the children become the leaders in the battle against the evil White Witch and, ultimately, her defeat. In the end Lucy becomes Queen Lucy the Valiant and stays in Narnia.

Jesus was clear that the kingdom of God requires childlike faith. "He called a little child to him, and placed the child among them. And he said: 'Truly I tell you, unless you change and become like little children, you will never enter the kingdom of heaven. Therefore, whoever takes the lowly position of this child is the greatest in the kingdom of heaven'" (Matt 18:20-24). One of the greatest challenges for successful businessmen and businesswomen is to live by faith and not by sight. After years of decisions made based on investment principles, the stock market, and wealth management, trusting God's ways more than man's ways is extremely difficult. In God's commonwealth common sense can often be the enemy of faith. God's ways are not our ways. "Now faith is the substance of being sure of what we hope for and certain of what we do not see" (Heb 11:2). The more we trust, the more we see, even when we have doubts. We must remember that God's kingdom is much more than our kingdom. "And we know that all things work together for good to those who love God, to those who are the called according to His purpose" (Rom 8:28).

A Moral Compass Based on God's Priorities

To be sanctified means to be "set apart." Once a child of God begins to see himself through God's eyes, one's philosophy of life becomes scrutinized. The core values that drive one's actions and thoughts often change in light of the reexamined life. What matters? How do I spend my time? Who do I really love? How do I show it? What do I do with my possessions? While it is natural for many to wander through life with an existential approach with little attention to an organized value system, a godly life demands a godly worldview. In a postmodern culture, millennials are noted for their uncertainty of what they want or where they are going, often living by momentary feelings or the influence of what others think. Western values frequently focus on hedonistic desires to seek pleasure or Epicurean sensuality that think financial privilege is their doorway. Even Christians often discover their values may be "Christianized," but not truly "Christian." While sometimes guided by traditional religious norms about right and wrong, many seem to waffle somewhere between cultural expectations and a loose Judeo-Christian code, being inconsistent with both views.

"Evidence suggests that people who have a healthy functioning moral compass are more grounded, focused, content with life and productive. They also seem to have more nurturing and positive relationships with people around them and their environment. They minimize harm to this world and maximize their contributions. In other words, they give back as much as they take in or maybe even more. They also have a healthier sense of individualistic self, while concentrating on a good for all" (Rad 2011). Developing a deeper moral compass also deepens one's integrity, self-confidence, and direction to make choices consistent with internalized beliefs.

Christianity offers such a moral compass. Followers of Jesus for centuries have recognized his life and teachings as a superior way to live and make choices. Even respected non-Christians like India's Mahatma Gandhi have affirmed the ethics of the New Testament as a guide. Ideas such as loving one's enemies, doing good to those who hurt you, forgiving others who do not deserve it, giving sacrificially, and laying down one's own desires and needs for another are praised. The lifestyle of Jesus was radical in the face of his own culture and still is for our culture.

Choosing and deepening a Christian philosophy of life, a moral compass, is an important sign of maturity because it involves critical thinking about one's ability and desire to bless others. Those who are committed to a Christian worldview can find guides in the Bible to direct and deepen their journey toward selflessness. These values will be constantly challenged with compromises that quickly erode their impact, but over time and with more consistency the values become stronger and saying "no" or "yes" becomes a clearer daily choice.

One of the byproducts of living out this moral compass is the joy it brings. There is even proof. While having money does not bring happiness, it has long been acknowledged that acts of generosity raise levels of happiness and emotional well being, giving charitable people a pleasant feeling known in behavioral economics as a "warm glow." There are studies that show that giving to others actually activates an area of the brain linked with contentment and the reward cycle. The decision to give makes us happier, and even though it is costly, it is beneficial. "It was also found that all participants who had performed, or had been willing to perform, an act of generosity—no matter how small—viewed themselves as happier at the end of the experiment. You don't need to become a self-sacrificing martyr to feel happier. Just being a little more generous will suffice" (Tobler 2017).

Happiness, however, seems to diminish for the rich over time. The pursuit of wealth becomes addictive, even when there is more than enough to meet one's needs. In over two thousand

interviews with millionaires, Harvard Business School professor
Michael Norton found that "all the way up the income-wealth
spectrum, basically everyone says [they'd need] two or three
times as much to be perfectly happy" (Pinsker 2018).

"Woe to you who are rich," said Jesus in the Sermon on the
Mount. It was a constant warning that money and riches can
destroy us. Desiring more is addictive and seductive, and adver-
tisers never relent from their pleas to get the next thing. Without
a deep moral discernment in place, materialism literally starves
the soul. An undisciplined, wanton lifestyle corrupts priorities
and relationships. We become the spoiled child who think the
world lives for our every need.

Mobilize

In reality, fear often inhibits steps outside one's natural past and
the newly adopted philosophy of life. The good news is that
there are simple and profound ways to deepen Christian values. At Mission Waco we learned years ago that the mobilizing
process is a long, slow process and must begin where the participant is, not where we wish they were. Having come out of a
stagnant church world, I understand the thinking patterns and
fears of institutionalized Christians to personally get involved
with the poor and marginalized. The Bible study at the church
building feels safe, even when the content of studying Jesus' life
is not. Stepping outside that comfort zone into the streets of
one's community to do the work Jesus called us to do may not
be as comfortable.

Years ago I discovered that the first step could be seeking
opportunities to go to other churches and speak in their Sunday School classes, worship services, small groups, retreats, or
conferences. Since it is our story of change I can tell the decisions and experiences of how God led us outside the walls of
cultural Christianity to a world in need. I share the joys, challenges, and stories of real people and our love for them. Then I
can invite them to join me for a ninety-minute bus ride at Mission Waco. In most instances up to one third of those invited

will actually take Mission Waco's bus ride through the streets and neighborhoods of Waco to see the areas which most have never seen. They are given a twenty-question quiz about poverty, local demographics, and services for the poor in Waco. During the tour all of those questions are answered and sometimes discussed as we ride. "What is the poverty threshold in America?" "What is the median income in Waco?" "What is the percent of racial minorities, the poor, the unemployed, and the mentally ill in your/our city?" "How much is the minimum wage?" "Where do the homeless sleep?" We take time at the end of the tour to answer and clarify those questions. And then it happens: as they exit the nonthreatening ride, many of them will ask, "How can I get plugged in?"

Next steps are crucial for the neophyte who is seeking to grow. Our experience is that a few, clearly defined, one-time opportunities are critical. For example, we ask if they would like to cook a meal for the homeless, attend a devotional at the shelter, or bring cookies for the children's program. To whatever degree possible, we seek to ask the first-time volunteers how that activity went for them and what they learned. Frequently they will then ask if they can volunteer on some kind of ongoing basis. We almost always have volunteer applications ready to hand out. And then we watch God's gentle hand move them deeper into a world they never imagined themselves serving in.

Volunteer

While volunteering is a great way to engage the wealthy with the poor and marginalized, there are some challenges. Like most of us in the dominant culture, we want to "fix" things and people. Both individuals and groups often think they see and understand the issues of poverty without ever having listened to those they want to help. They can quickly come up with a list of things they want to do "for them," not "with them." Helping is relational. Relationships take time and are built on dignity and mutuality. The volunteer who has an immediate need to fix the person or problem can often become a bigger problem to the organization. Training is necessary for them to be effective, and often a listening volunteer will realize for the first time that their own presuppositions about how they want to help others are part of a larger paternalistic approach which actually disempowers the poor. Poverty of spirit is a critical characteristic and value for the volunteer.

There are numerous opportunities for Americans to volunteer, each with varying degrees of impact. Our focus is on finding sites where interaction with those served can become a mutual experience. For example, serving a meal to the poor may be important, but conversations that happen during a devotional at a homeless shelter offer more opportunity for discussion. From playing games with children in a backyard Bible club in a housing complex to helping the sick in a free clinic, God's Spirit seems to prod our thinking to new heights of compassion.

More than just serving in another feeding program, volunteers with unique gifts that influence policy and create wealth are critical to overcome poverty. To combat deeper causes of poverty in lower-income neighborhoods, two particular strategies are needed. "On the one hand, we should challenge the systemic forces that contribute to the creation and maintenance of poverty. On the other hand, social enterprise must become a larger part of the overall strategy" (James 2013, 163). The legal and business world can offer crucial help. Lawyers can direct efforts of impacting public policy and advocate for the poor in their cities, states, and nation. Professionals with business administration, finance, and entrepreneurial skills can guide community development projects with mature and sustainable nonprofits in the urban centers. Skilled fundraisers can help struggling urban ministries develop better strategies than car washes and garage sales. Professors and graduate students can research data that supports grants or seek out the best practices of what other successful nonprofits are doing nationwide. They can also develop and analyze surveys that inform community leaders of the realities of their local poor and marginalized populations. Most every profession has expertise that can undergird poverty alleviation.

Read Books That Push You

For those who are more uncertain about diving in, there are numerous books that can stir one's heart to consider the journey of engagement. Several years ago, a life-changing story called *Same Kind of Different as Me* by Ron Hall and Denver Moore shared the story of a millionaire art dealer who was dragged by his wife to serve a meal to the homeless, and one of the homeless men in the food line became his friend. As their awkward friendship developed over the weeks, an amazing bond developed that changed both men.

In the book *Nickeled and Dimed: On Not Getting Along in America*, Barbara Ehrenreich shows how hard it is to make it, let alone get ahead, on low wages in America. It is a wake-up call for people who think a job, any job, is the answer to getting out of poverty or financial insecurity. Most of the poor work at least two jobs, and some work three or more. It shows how unfair this system is and how it works against low-wage workers.

Educator and author Ruby Payne's books *A Framework for Understanding Poverty: A Cognitive Approach* and *Bridges Out of Poverty* have impacted millions of practitioners to understand the mindset of the poor and help from their perspective instead of commonly held presuppositions.

Books such as *When Helping Hurts: How to Alleviate Poverty Without Hurting the Poor . . . and Yourself* by Corbett and Fikkert and *Toxic Charity* by Robert Lupton help naïve volunteers see the danger of "cheap charity," which often hurts the poor and hinders their own responsibility. Learning when to offer relief and when to push others toward empowerment is important for maturing volunteerism.

Attend a Conference . . . Create a Conference

Education and awareness are critical roles of nonprofits to inform their communities of the challenges and needs in their own cities. Unfortunately, many compassionate local ministries are overworked and undertrained to address the challenges in their communities. Networking with other nonprofits offers a way to bring new hope and skills.

After years of attending the national Christian Community Development Association conference, several Texas Christian pioneers began to ask how we could increase the numbers of practitioners in our own state who knew the principles of Christian community development and, therefore, could create more vital ministries to empower the poor. In 2010 Mission Waco held its first conference by bringing in three speakers to discuss three issues that affect the poor. We were surprised at the response, both in number and content quality. Over the next two years we saw the "No Need Among You" (Deut 15:4) conference grow. To seek God's direction we gathered several urban ministry leaders together to listen to their thoughts and determine our plans for the future. We concluded there was genuine need and support for a full-blown statewide conference and organization in Texas. In 2013 the Texas Christian Community Development Network (TxCCDN) was approved as a 501c3 tax-exempt nonprofit organization to be led by a board of directors from seven regions of the State with this expressed purpose: "Based on God's incarnational love through Jesus Christ, the Texas Christian Community Development Network (TxCCDN) is called to bring healing and hope to disadvantaged communities, neighborhoods and residents of the Lone Star State by connecting, educating, training and advocating for the poor and marginalized in Texas." The organization now has two codirectors and a coordinator to organize the annual conference, as well as plan workshops held in various Texas cities and several one-day training sessions in random locations.

As this and other movements grow there is an increasing desire to address issues of all kinds through local neighborhood groups, national advocacy organizations, and global ministries. Volunteers are discovering that their particular passions for the poor and marginalized and the need for the gifts God gave them to address those concerns have places to be used like never before.

Short-Term Exposure Trips

There is something about seeing, smelling, and touching that is more life-changing than just hearing. Yet many committed Christians have never ventured out very far beyond their own areas of the communities, much less into the world of need. They may have heard about poverty in their city or seen a news story on it, but to actually journey into those circumstances brings up fears that are often unfounded. With some on-site awareness in their places of security, a good mobilizer can help Christians move from the church building into their own communities, even to other countries where poverty is compounded. Repetition and listening to their concerns may eventually motivate small steps. While the pool of potential traditional Christians may shrink as the mobilizing experience deepens in impact, nonetheless it is worth the cost to offer increasing exposure to the poor of our nation and world to those who are ready and willing. For over thirty-years we have taken hundreds of Christians to Mexico City, Haiti, and India. Each trip is purposely different. Mexico City is the easiest of the three. With a population of some 30 million inhabitants, the size and numbers are overwhelming. We stay in a middle-income hotel, eat and drink safe food and water, and take day trips to a ministry site with which we are very familiar. Along with our Mexican friends, we go to an orphanage with over two hundred mentally and physically disabled children. We attend a Christian gathering in an impoverished barrio in the backyard of their leader to sing, pray and eat together. We go to a homeless shelter with over five hundred men to sing and fellowship. On Sunday morning we worship with a "sister church" that our own Church Under the Bridge supports. It is an incredible first step into a world that most American Christians have never imagined.

The exposure trip to Haiti is much different because their poverty is even more extreme. The average Haitian earns less than one dollar a day and struggles to live. For the American participants who get to play with the children we support to attend school, or meet the women in the micro-credit loan program who have successfully grown a small business that supports their family, or be at the site of a new water well that spurts forth life-giving water, there develops a brand new perspective on the poor. For the first time many of them wonder what it would be like to not be able to feed their own children or teach them to read. They come to admire those who are working as hard as they can for so little money. They begin to realize their own privilege to drink clean water, access a doctor, or not have to walk ten miles by foot to a destination. They realize the value of empowering others instead of quick-fix solutions.

India is vast and a very different culture with numerous religions, the Taj Mahal and leper slums. Mission World has focused mostly on a Muslim tribal group of about two million poor who live mostly in North India. They are buffalo herders, some of whom traverse the mountainous area of the Himalayan foothills during certain times of the year. They sell the buffalo milk in their small communities and struggle to eke out a living. Many are afraid of the dominant Hindu culture that typically despises them. Some of our trips have helped them find access to healthcare, which most of whom do not have access to. Participants who go on this longer exposure trip get to trek in the mountains with them, stay in a small village, and visit Hindu and Buddhist temples, as well as tour popular sites in India. Participants seek to understand Eastern worldviews and how those adherents look at issues of poverty and suffering. Obviously this trip challenges Christians in ways unlike the others.

Growing Compassion among the Wealthy

One of our great joys is watching wealthy Christians grow. For example, we have watched a millionaire woman in our ministry, who has chosen to travel with us to both Haiti and Mexico City, be changed as she has seen the challenges of extreme poverty. She has held disabled orphans in her arms and danced with those who could walk. She annually helps send relief to the orphans. A millionaire couple has used their private airplane numerous times to fly food and helpers like us to devasted hurricane victims in poor countries. After the death of her wealthy husband, another millionaire widow began to advocate for other widows and wrote a book to help them adjust to the changes of life without a spouse. She became a strong advocate for the racial minorities near her city who received less assistance than others during a devastating hurricane recovery effort. Hundreds of our middle-class donors have chosen to become school sponsors for the poor children in our work who otherwise could not attend school. Others pledged critical startup funds for women's microcredit loans or helped purchase a water well drilling rig so clean water could replace the unfiltered river water that was killing village children. Medical teams not only have served with us in other countries but in our local free clinic, using their expertise to help those without access to healthcare.

In our hometown, one wealthy lawyer goes each week to a low-performing public school to help "his" second-grader practice reading. A wealthy businesswoman donated a rent house in our part of town to house college interns so they can come live and learn for extended periods of time how to best serve the poor. Several pastors have joined with Pastors for Public School to advocate to State Congressmen for better support for poorer schools. Over fifty churches annually cook and serve meals to the homeless in the community. Businessmen and women have joined together as mentors to assist unemployed men and women to refine workplace skills in order to get and keep jobs. Others lead discussions and Bible studies at local homeless shelters. Hundreds more have participated in an annual "Walk for the Homeless" that educates the community about their needs. There are volunteer lawyers who provide legal advice for the poor who cannot otherwise access help. Some banks have sent trained employees to help guide the poor to overcome indebtedness and bad credit ratings so that they could qualify for affordable housing. Committees across the community have engaged persons of influence to shape community opportunities for former inmates returning to start over in their cities. Especially important to ex-offenders is getting jobs that otherwise would not be available to those with a criminal past.

In many cases engaging the wealthy in the specific challenges of the poor gives them insights to the complexity of poverty and more informed possibilities for transformation. Instead of simplistic fixes which rarely work, those who sit on the boards of nonprofits or local community advocacy groups become informed leaders. Often their money follows their engagement to support realistic solutions they now understand.

Back to Zacchaeus

The cost of the chief tax collector's decision to repent and follow Jesus was financially expensive. Giving up half of his income to the poor and paying four times back to those he had cheated was no small decision. His confession could have been considered an admission to crime. It certainly made difficult his relationship with other publicans and even Rome itself. Based on the story of Zacchaeus, salvation in God's kingdom came with guidelines of how followers of Jesus approached wealth. Generosity to the poor and giving to the needs of the community were not optional for a Christian, but implicit in a regenerated life. Salvation was not just personal, but had communal responsibility and privilege. Furthermore, such acts of sacrificial compassion by Zacchaeus and other early believers influenced others in their cities to understand the transformative nature of the gospel on every aspect of life, that "all may see the salvation of God" (Luke 3:6). Jesus' encounter with the publican reminds us that Christian faith has social implications which may widen our narrow views, helping us realize that "the sinner's prayer" is not only for a future heaven. Zacchaeus' response to Jesus included practical steps with his money in the presence of Jesus and in the community where he lived.

Christian community development gives wings to Isaiah's call to "rebuild," "restore," and "renew" our neighborhoods. Whether by sacrificial generosity, advocacy for the poor in the halls of government, or using the talents and gifts we have been given to empower others, we are to be "doers of the word, not hearers only" (Jas 1:27).

One of the joys that Christians experience is involvement in their own communities to empower the poor, sustain the good work of nonprofit organizations and churches, use their unique skills, and dream larger dreams that benefit the whole community. Like Zacchaeus, with a redeemed moral compass and the Spirit's power we become free from our selfishness and narcissism to turn our focus on our neighbors instead of ourselves. Things "on earth" that affect the disenfranchised become our issues too. The gifts God gives us become tools to be used for the Father's sake for our brothers and sisters.

Planned Giving

Because many wealthy and middle-class Christians often live a carefree life, their spending patterns tend to be more random. They often have certain charities they prefer, and they give to them as funds allow, including tax benefits for their donations. Others are more intentional, desiring a portfolio to guide their decisions. To maximize personal wealth some Christians prefer to work through licensed financial advisors who understand the world of money and various ways to increase the funds of their clients. Donor advised funds have become more popular in recent years because the wealthy can receive an immediate deduction on their taxes for the amount they have "donated" by depositing into the fund, and when they are ready to make their donation, which could be years in the future, they alert the fund and their money will be disbursed to the cause of their choosing. Unlike personal foundations, which usually give 5 percent of their income away to nonprofits, donor advised funds give around 20 percent and are much easier to administer.

Groups like the National Christian Foundation have also become recognized guides for those wishing to donate not just funds but property, privately held stock, business interests, tangible personal property, life insurance, and royalties. Since

1982 they have funneled 11 billion dollars in grants to some 63,000 charities.

Instead of random and futile donations given mostly at the year's end, the financially blessed ones make money to give it away. They plan in advance to fulfill their dreams of God's kingdom and of those visions that God has given to those whom they feel compelled to support. They are blessed to bless.

The Graduated Tithe

Random givers typically give less than they can. Some estimates are that today "born-again Christians" give about 2.2 percent of their gross income; about 4 percent of Christians tithe. In his book *Rich Christians in an Age of Hunger* Dr. Ron Sider suggests that if Christians gave a full tithe, based on the Old Testament Law, i.e., 10 percent of their income, there would be enough private Christian dollars to provide basic healthcare and education for all the poor of the earth, with millions more leftover for missional work. Even if those amounts had withstood inflation, the reality is that most believers give far less than a tithe. Following a global pandemic, most likely the amount will decrease even more.

The New Testament does not clearly push the tithe as the standard of giving, but actually goes much farther. Early Christians, often considered social radicals, are described in Acts as sharing everything they had, selling property and possessions, and giving to anyone who had need. Today's church would never consider such an approach.

Another way to guide "how much" one should give is called the "graduated tithe." This strategy is simple. As one's income increases, one's giving should increase. Seeking to always avoid legalism, a natural way to give out of one's changing annual income would start with a base amount. For example, $40,000 might work for a low-middle income family, based on the family's size, plus costs for education and college expenses, plus taxes and genuine emergencies. The family tries to give 10 percent of that base amount. Then, for each $1,000 of income above that base amount, they give an additional 5 percent. An example might help:

Income	% to Give	$ to Give	Total Income	Total $ Given	Total % Given
$40,000	10%	$4000	$40,000	$4000	10%
Next $1000	15%	$150	$41,000	$4150	10.1%
Next $1000	20%	$200	$42,000	$4350	10.4%
Next $1000	25%	$250	$43,000	$4600	10.7%

After you reach a total income of $57,000, you'll be giving away 100 percent of any additional money you earn. If your income was $75,000, you'd be giving $31,350 under this system—a little over 40 percent. At $100,000, you'd be giving away $56,350 or just over 56 percent.

The advantage of the graduated tithe is that it helps avoid extra, and often foolish, spending with increased income. Increasing your wealth, therefore, blesses others in a strategic way. While any Christian can choose to give more generously each year, this model offers at least one way to approach it. One of the more radical approaches is to give away everything beyond the annual median income in the United States and live at that same income. The median income in the U.S. was $61,372 in 2018. Obviously such a decision would change the lifestyles of thousands of Christians, but also bless thousands more.

A person or family's strategy to being generous may vary, but since most Americans do not even have a strategy, the decision process alone is important to awaken God's call to bless others. Without rails to guide their giving, many Christians give little to the church or to the poor and marginalized, considering random acts of giving adequate. God's call to Abraham was that we are blessed to bless. While the Scripture reminds us that "to much is given, much will be required," the joy of giving generously has little to do with requirements or tithes, but with privilege. We get to give.

The Giving Pledge of the Super Rich

There are those in our nation and world who are financially blessed beyond any comprehension of most people. While
there are movies and legends about the super wealthy that tell
their tales, there is another group of billionaires that have cap-
tured the attention of our materialistic and greedy world that
defy what many think could happen. They are generously giving
to the needs of the poor and those suffering around the world.
Some are donating as much as 99 percent of their wealth.

In August of 2010, forty of America's wealthiest people joined
together in a commitment to give the majority of their wealth to
address some of society's most pressing problems. Created by Bill
and Melinda Gates and Warren Buffett, The Giving Pledge came
to life following a series of conversations with philanthropists
around the world about how they could collectively set a new
standard of generosity among the ultra-wealthy. By 2018 The
Giving Pledge had been signed by forty billionaires along with
175 of the world's wealthiest people from twenty-two countries.
These ultra-rich men and women have committed to giving away
more than half of their wealth to global causes such as poverty
alleviation, refugee aid, disaster relief, global health, education,
women and girls' empowerment, medical research, arts and culture, criminal justice reform, and environmental sustainability.
Mega-billionaires like American businessman Warren Buffett
and Microsoft's Bill and Melinda Gates are passionately living
out their lives by encouraging the world's super-wealthy to join
in the pledge. "With wealth comes responsibility to help make
the world a better place," says media mogul Ted Turner. Warren
Buffet has taken the pledge to another level, committing to give
away 99 percent of his current $45 billion fortune. The Gates
have agreed to give away the vast amount of their $54 billion
empire through their foundation, acting also as salesmen to encourage others to join The Giving Pledge. They know that when
people know that other people are aware of their giving, their
donations rise as much as fourfold.

Mackenzie Bezos, the ex-wife of Amazon's Jeff Bezos, said, "There are lots of resources each of us can pull from our safes to share with other . . . time, attention, knowledge, patience, creativity, talent, effort, humor, compassion. In addition to whatever assets life has nurtured in me, I have a disproportionate amount of money to share. My approach to philanthropy will continue to be thoughtful. It will take time and effort and care. But it won't wait. And I will keep at it until the safe is empty" (The Giving Pledge 2019).

In some curious and ironic ways, these super wealthy folks have discovered what millions of ordinary, lukewarm Christians have not yet found: the privilege and call to care for the poor locally and globally. While they certainly will never experience hunger themselves, they have learned the eternal value of giving. For example, the Bill and Melinda Gates Foundation spends $2 billion a year on aiding Africa alone, largely to improve health and agriculture with access to vaccines and more productive seeds. When others complain about "donor fatigue," giving to causes that seem to never succeed, Gates reminds the cynics that in the last twenty years childhood death in Africa has been cut in half, and deaths from HIV are half of what they were at their peak. Even deaths from malaria are half of what they were a few years ago. He and his wife know this because they dived deeply into relationships for years with Africans to learn together how to attack the evil of poverty. While there is more to do, they are doing remarkable things.

While the spiritual lives of these "rich and famous" folks are rarely publicly acknowledged for their generosity, it seems they have discovered the fruits of God's principles of compassion and sacrifice. Whether they know him as the source, their hearts seem ripe for the Spirit's clarion call. While only God himself will be their ultimate judge, it is clear that many of them can at least answer Jesus' question, "When did you see them hungry, or thirsty, or sick, or naked, or in prison?" Many have seen and many of them have responded like "sheep," unlike the "goats" who were condemned.

The Giving Lifestyle of the Super Poor

At the other end of the financial grid from the super rich was a very poor widow that Jesus noticed one day among the clamor of the temple. "As Jesus looked up, he saw the rich putting their gifts into the temple treasury. He also saw a poor widow put in two very small copper coins. 'Truly I tell you,' he said, 'this poor widow has put in more than all the others. All these people gave their gifts out of their wealth; but she out of her poverty put in all she had to live on'" (Luke 21:1-4). To "give out of our poverty" is the greatest and most godly way to give and live. In Christian theology the basis of salvation and following Christ is based in emptying oneself (*kenosis*) from all other gods and all selfishness, and become entirely receptive to the Father's divine will. The Apostle Paul recognized this remarkable ethic in Jesus life with others, saying, "In your relationships with one another, have the same mindset as Christ Jesus: Who, being in very nature God, did not consider equality with God something to be used to his own advantage; rather, he made himself nothing by taking the very nature of a servant, being made in human likeness" (Phil 2:5-7). Spiritual poverty is that deep awareness that we are nothing compared to the Father, Son, and Holy Spirit. It is from him we receive our value, our purpose, our example, and our being. "For God so loved the world he gave . . ." (John 3:16).

BIBLIOGRAPHY

Alcorn, Randy. 1989. *Money, Possessions, and Eternity*. Wheaton, Ill.: Tyndale House.

Alighieri, Dante. 1982. *The Divine Comedy of Dante Alighieri: Inferno*. New York City: Random House.

The Aspen Institute. 2020. Weave: The Social Fabric Project. https://www.aspeninstitute.org/programs/weave-the-social-fabric-initiative/.

Assari, Shervin. 2017. "Why Poverty Is Not a Personal Choice but a Reflection of Society." *The Conversation*, June 30.

Atlas of Giving. 2016. *July 2016 Report*. Dallas: Philanthropy News Digest.

Bailey, Sarah Pulliam. 2019. "In U.S., Decline of Christianity Continues at Rapid Pace: An Update on America's Changing Religious Landscape." *Washington Post*, November 15.

Blomberg, Craig L. 1997. *Jesus and the Gospels: An Introduction and Survey*. Nashville: B&H.

Bosch, David J. 2014. *Transforming Mission: Paradigm Shifts in Theology of Mission*. Maryknoll, N.Y.: Orbis.

Brooks, David. 2019. *The Second Mountain: The Quest for a Moral Life*. New York: Random House.

Bunyan, John. 1998. *The Pilgrim's Progress in Modern English*. Edited by L. Edward Hazelbaker. Alachua, Fla.: Bridge-Logos Publishing.

Chan, Francis, and Preston Sprinkle. 2011. *Erasing Hell: What God Said about Eternity and the Things We Made Up.* Colorado Springs: David C. Cook.

Chronicle of Philanthropy and Graham-Pelton Consulting Firm. 2013. "How America Gives: A Recent Report from Graham-Pelton Highlights the Changing Giving Habits of Americans and How Some Nonprofits Are Adjusting Their Strategies in the Face of Declining Middle-Class Donors." In *Diagnostic and Statistical Manual of Mental Disorders.* 5th ed. Washington, D.C.: American Psychiatric Association.

Cohut, Maria. 2017. "Generosity Makes You Happier." *Medical News Today*, July 16.

Corbett, Steve, and Fikkert, Brian. 2009. *When Helping Hurts: How to Alleviate Poverty without Hurting the Poor and Yourself.* Chicago: Moody Publishers.

Dorrell, Jimmy, and Janet Dorrell. 2006. *Plunge2Poverty: An Intensive Poverty Simulation Experience.* Birmingham: New Hope Publishers.

———. 2006. *Trolls and Truth: 14 Realities about Today's Church That We Don't Want to See.* Birmingham: New Hope Publishers.

Ehrenreich, Barbara. 2011. *Nickel and Dimed: On (Not) Getting by in America.* New York: Picador.

Gillman, John. 1991. *Possessions and the Life of Faith: A Reading of Luke-Acts.* Collegeville, Minn.: Liturgical Press.

The Giving Pledge. 2019. https://givingpledge.org/Pledger.aspx?id =393.

Granberg-Michaelson, Wesley. 2019. "Where Is Christianity Headed from 2019?" *Black Christian News Network One*, January 10.

Green, Gary Paul, and Anna Haines. 2008. *Asset Building and Community Development.* 2nd ed. Thousand Oaks, Calif.: Sage.

Hall, Ron, and Denver Moore. 2008. *Same Kind of Different as Me.* Nashville: Thomas Nelson.

Harries, Richard. 1992. *Is There a Gospel for the Rich? The Christian in a Capitalist World.* London: Mowbray.

Hays, Christopher M. *Luke's Wealth Ethics.* Tubingen, Germany: Mohr Siebeck, 2010.

Hinson-Hasty, Elizabeth L. 2017. *The Problem of Wealth: A Christian Response to the Culture of Affluence.* Maryknoll, N.Y.: Orbis.

Holman, Susan R., ed. 2008. *Wealth and Poverty in the Early Church and Society.* Grand Rapids: Baker Academic.

Ingraham, Christopher. 2019. "Wealth Deficit Dire for Millennials." *Washington Post,* December 3.

Inoue, Takanori. 2017. *The Early Church's Approach to the Poor in Society and Its Significance to the Church's Social Engagement Today.* Research paper, Asbury Theological Seminary.

James, Larry M. 2013. *The Wealth of the Poor.* Abilene: ACU Press.

Kahan, Alan S. 2009. *Mind vs. Money: The War between Intellectuals and Capitalism.* Piscataway, N.J.: Transaction Publishers.

Kochhar, Rakesh. 2018. "The American Middle Class Is Stable in Size, but Losing Ground Financially to Upper-Income Families." Pew Research Center, September 6.

The Lausanne Movement. 1974. *The Lausanne Covenant.* https://www.lausanne.org/content/covenant/lausanne-covenant#cov.

Lewis, C. S. 1998. *The Lion, the Witch and the Wardrobe.* New York: HarperCollins.

———. 2015. *The Great Divorce.* San Francisco: HarperOne.

Lincoln, Ryan, Christopher A. Morrissey, and Peter Mundey. 2008. "Religious Giving: A Comprehensive Review of the Literature." *The Science of Generosity Initiative,* University of Notre Dame.

Linthicum, Robert C. 2006. *Building a People of Power: Equipping Churches to Transform Their Communities.* Waynesboro, Ga.: Authentic in partnership with World Vision.

Lupton, Robert D. 2012. *Toxic Charity: How Churches and Charities Hurt Those They Help and How to Reverse It.* San Francisco: HarperOne.

Metzger, James A. 2007. *Consumption and Wealth in Luke's Travel Narrative.* Leiden: Brill.

Moberg, David O. 1972. *The Great Reversal: Evangelism versus Social Concern.* Philadelphia: Lippincott.

Myers, Bryant L. 1999. *Walking with the Poor: Principles and Practices of Transformational Development.* Maryknoll, N.Y.: Orbis.

Mullin, Redmond. 1984. *The Wealth of Christians*. Maryknoll, N.Y.: Orbis.

Nelson, Mary. 2010. *Empowerment: A Key Component to Christian Community Development*. Christian Community Development Association.

Payne, Ruby K. 2009. *Bridges Out of Poverty: Strategies for Professionals and Communities*. Highlands, Tex.: aha! Process Publishing.

———. 2018. *A Framework for Understanding Poverty: A Cognitive Approach*. 6th ed. Highlands, Tex.: aha! Process Publishing.

Peck, M. Scott. 1998. *A Different Drum: Community Making and Peace*. New York: Simon and Schuster.

Peterson, Eugene H. 2007. *The Message Bible*. Colorado Springs: NavPress.

Philanthropy News Digest. 2016. "Gates Foundation to Invest $5 Billion in Africa over Five Years." July 19. https://philanthropynewsdigest.org/news/gates-foundation-to-invest-5-billion-in-africa-over-five-years.

Pinsker, Joe. 2018. "The Reason Many Ultrarich People Aren't Satisfied with Their Wealth." *Atlantic*, December 4.

Powys, David. *"Hell": A Hard Look at a Hard Question: The Fate of the Unrighteous in New Testament Thought*. Waynesboro, Ga.: Paternoster, 1997.

Rad, Michelle Roya. 2011. "How to Deal with Self-Centered People." *Huffington Post*, December 3.

Rhee, Helen. 2012. *Loving the Poor, Saving the Rich: Wealth, Poverty, and Early Christian Formation*. Grand Rapids: Baker Academic.

Rosenberg, Yuval. 2012. "You Need a $150,000 Income to Lead a Good Life in America." *Business Insider*, March 7.

Sample, Tex. 1993. *Hard Living People and Mainstream Christians*. Nashville: Abingdon.

Schervish, Paul G., and Keith Whitaker. 2010. *Wealth and the Will of God: Discerning the Use of Riches in the Service of Ultimate Purposes*. Bloomington: Indiana University Press.

Sider, Ronald J. 2015. *Rich Christians in an Age of Hunger: Moving Affluence to Generosity*. 6th ed. Grand Rapids: W Publishing Group, 2015.

Simon, Arthur. 2003. *How Much Is Enough? Hungering for God in an Affluent Culture*. Grand Rapids: Baker.

Smith, Christian, and Michael Emerson. 2008. *Passing the Plate: Why American Christians Aren't More Generous*. New York: Oxford University Press.

Snyder, Anne. 2019. *The Fabric of Character: A Wise Giver's Guide to Supporting Social and Moral Renewal*. Washington, D.C.: The Philanthropy Roundtable.

Stark, Rodney. 1996. *The Rise of Christianity: A Sociologist Reconsiders History*. Princeton, N.J.: Princeton University Press.

Taylor, Michael. 2003. *Christianity, Poverty and Wealth: The Findings of "Project 21."* London: WCC Publications.

Thorbecke, Catherine. 2019. "Nearly Half of the World's Entire Wealth Is in the Hands of Millionaires: The Credit Suisse Global Wealth Report." *ABC News*, October 22.

Ware, Andy. 2018. "Fewer Americans Are Giving Money to Charity but Total Donations Are at Record Levels Anyway." Lilly Foundation, July 12.

Wealth-X Billionaire Census. 2019. https://www.wealthx.com/report/the-wealth-xbillionaire-census-2019/.

Printed in the USA
CPSIA information can be obtained
at www.ICGtesting.com
CBHW021720180224
4434CB00001B/104

9 781481 31350